Padre Pio...
The Capuchin

The Life & Times of St. Pio of Pietrelcina

Sex, Horror & Violence

vs.

Unyielding Faith!

By
Othniel J. Seiden

A Books to Believe In Publication

Cover Design
Capri Brock
DesignsByCapri.com

ISBN: 1519495684

Table of Contents

Table of Contents

Table of Contents

On September 20th, 1928, in a monastery hidden hight in the hills of Southern Italy, something very strange happened to a certain Capuchin monk.

Alarmed by the unexplainable events which began to follow, the Church ordered his immediate confinement. But even the thick stone walls of his cell could not detain the phenomenal forces that surrounded him. In a very short time, the entire countryside was keenly aware of his presence. And now, the World will know…

Author's Note

This story is based on the true facts of Padre Pio's life. Some of the events herein are composites of events that have been documented by numerous and reliable sources. Readers who are doubtful, or those who wish to delve further into the story of Padre Pio's life, are referred to the numerous writings about this remarkable Capuchin friar-priest, some listed at the end of this book. Since many of the people involved in Padre Pio's life may still be alive, some of their names have been changed. A few of the characters are also fictitious.

The person who reads this novel and then explores this religious man further will discover that the real life of Padre Pio is far more remarkable and fantastic than any product of this writer's imagination. Many of the anecdotes are difficult to believe, and I present them as a reporter, for you to determine believability for yourself. However, these stories have been researched, in an attempted to be disproved by many, including the Vatican. Though some could not be verified, they could not be disproven.

I now respectfully submit my story of Padre Pio, the Capuchin...,

Othniel J. Seiden

Part I.

The Capuchin

Chapter 1

Upon entering a chapel no one would expect to find a man lying in a pool of fresh blood at the foot of the altar, especially not the priest. But that is what occurred when **Brother Nicola** went in search of **Padre Pio** on the morning of September 20, 1918.

It was still very early morning. The sun was just beginning to play through the stained glass of the chapel. Already the monks of the monastery at **San Giovanni Rotondo** had been up and attending to their duties for several hours. The monastery and its church, **Saint Mary of Graces**, were nestled high in the **Gargano Mountains**, overlooking the **Gulf of Manfredonia** in southern Italy. A snaking mountain road led a mile-and-a-half down from the monastery to the town of San Giovanni Rotondo.

As the rays of the new day's sun began to reflect on the dew-covered earth, the last howlings of the homeless dogs that constantly roamed the area died out. All night long the baying could be heard, and it had been that way as long as anyone could remember. Before the dogs, wolves had carried on the nightly lament. Now the wolves were fewer in number and they only occasionally replied to the dogs, but in a distinct and more commanding tone. The friars of Saint Mary of Graces were accustomed to the nightly sound and took pleasure in the break of the otherwise lonely silence. But they knew that it was unsafe to venture out of the great walls alone at night, and were gladdened that their duties rarely required treading outside the monastery walls even during the day, much less at night. The hungry animals ran in packs and could tear a single traveler to shreds.

Six friars and Padre Pio resided at the monastery. All but two were occupied at their studies or chores as that unforgettable day broke. Only Padre Pio and Brother Nicola were not with the others.

As had always been his habit, Padre Pio had risen in the first hours of the morning to pray in solitude. He'd gone to the chapel and entered through the small door that led to the back of the altar. There he had been kneeling before the large crucifix, entranced with his meditations, unaware of the worldly surroundings. He was feverish from the intensity of his prayer. Sweat poured off him, drenching his robes. He was oblivious to Brother Nicola passing the open door behind him.

Padre Pio had arrived at the monastery only four months earlier. He was sent there to die in peace. The frail padre had been plagued with ill health for the better part of his thirty-one years. When the **Father Guardian** had first asked that Brother Nicola keep a watchful eye on the sickly priest, there was a slight resentment. Playing nurse, he felt, was against his nature. He wondered if he'd be chasing bedpans most of the day. But the moment after the Father Guardian introduced Nicola to Pio, Pio whispered to Nicola, "Please be at peace. My illness is my burden, it is not for others to carry. And I pray that I will never need a bedpan. The only burden you will have is putting up with my bad jokes." Pio smiled at Nicola, and asked, "Can you show me to my suite?"

Brother Nicola was stunned by Pio's remark. *How did he know what I was thinking?* More than that, however, he was deeply embarrassed. Could this young monk read his innermost thoughts, or was it only a coincidence? Nonetheless, shame swept over him for his previous attitude. What right did he have to be reluctant to obey wholeheartedly the Father Guardian's request?

As Nicola led Pio to his crude cell, he noticed that Pio walked with an uncertain gait. Although Pio did an excellent job of hiding it on his face, Nicola realized he was in considerable pain, and Nicola's shame deepened.

In the weeks that followed, Pio kept his promise. He shied away from any special attention that was offered, and made light of Brother Nicola's constant shadowing of him. Embarrassed, Nicola decided to relax his vigil, but that was only to last three days. On the night of July 12, a whimpering, coming from the cell situated next to his, awakened Nicola. It was Pio's chamber. Rising quickly to his feet, he lit a candle and went to investigate. Just before opening Pio's door, he stopped short. The whimpering wasn't the only noise coming from within. There was another voice! No…not a voice, another presence…someone…or something…whispering. But such an unnatural sound! And now movement…a thud…a crash! Brother Nicola threw open the cell door. The corner of his eye caught the movement of a shadow near the small window on the opposite wall. Holding up his candle the light proved there was nothing there.

Pio was curled up on the floor. Nicola bent over and shined the light on his face. It was cut above the left eye, and bruised in several other places. The whimpering had subsided. Whatever threat had been here only a moment ago was now gone, Nicola thought. He shook the priest's shoulder.

"Pio…"

Pio responded by instantly shielding his face with his arms, and let out a small "yelp" like a frightened dog.

"Pio ...It's me, Nicola."

Pio peeked through his arms, as though not absolutely sure. Then he dropped his arms and began to cry, biting his lip to subdue the noise. Embarrassed, he allowed Nicola to help him onto his bed. "I'm sorry, Brother Nicola ... I'm afraid you're playing nurse after all. But I think it's too late for a bedpan," he said, as he looked down at his dampened robe.

"Pio ...What has happened here this night?"

Pio put his head down. "Just as my sickness, it is my battle. I was told it would be with me the rest of my mortal life."

"What battle? Who with? Who said it would always be with you?"

Pio's head remained down, and he said nothing. Nicola sensed Pio did not want to discuss it further. Many thoughts raced through Nicola's mind. *Surely these injuries were not self inflicted, but there was no one else in the room when I entered.* He remembered the shadow by the cell's window, but the window was far too small an opening for anyone to come in through. There was no doubt, though, about the second presence he sensed before entering the cell.

Both sat silent for what seemed like several minutes. "Is there anything I can do, Padre?" asked Nicola.

"Please sit with me ... at least for a little while." Pio didn't have to say that he was still frightened. He was obviously badly shaken.

Pio shortly fell into an exhausted sleep while Nicola sat in the small armless wooden chair at the foot of his bed. Nicola then got up, poured some water from the pitcher atop the crude washbasin onto his handkerchief, and preceded to cleanse the sleeping man's face. From now on, he would keep a much closer vigil.

The next morning, Pio's face was swollen, but by keeping the oversized hood of his robe over his head, he was able to avoid calling attention to his bruises until they disappeared a few days later.

During the weeks, which followed, Brother Nicola stayed very close, and at night left both his and Pio's doors ajar. But he always had to wait until Pio was asleep before cracking open his door, otherwise, his new ward would embarrassedly push it shut again.

Brother Nicola never mentioned the night of July 12 to the Father Guardian. It was his and Pio's secret, like a bond between the two men, and he prided himself on that. Although no more unexplainable incidences had occurred since then, there were occasions when Nicola would hear Pio talking to himself. It happened several different times, at any given hour of the day. But it was a strange way in which he mumbled to himself, because the conversation always seemed to be only one sided…as if another was there conversing with this unusual monk. The other monks, trained to be self-absorbed in their meditations, didn't seem to notice this, but Nicola did. Although during the first few months Pio had earned the reputation of being somewhat odd at times, all those residing at the friary respected him for the effort he put forth to perform his monastic duties. But to Nicola, Pio was more than "odd." Pio was something very special.

Chapter 2.

Brother Nicola knew it would be futile to try to get Padre Pio's attention before he finished his meditations. The wall could fall on the friar-priest and he wouldn't notice it. Nicola could barely make out the kneeling figure of the pious man in the dim light of the chapel. He continued past the door and looked out over the garden. Becoming absorbed in his own thoughts, several minutes passed before he returned to the door to see whether the padre had finished. Now the light had brightened as the sun penetrated the small window openings. The man was still kneeling.

"Good morning Padre Pio. You are feeling well this morning? There was no reply. Nicola was not surprised. A few minute more. Again he left the doorway, not to impede on the priest's solitude. He paced in the passageway a while longer. *If only I could pray as Pio does. So deep is his concentration, his communion.* This time when he returned to the open door the kneeling figure was gone. Nicola glanced around the room looking for his friend. *Has he slipped out unnoticed? He could not have. I'd have heard him, seen him.*

"Padre Pio? It is I, Nicola. Are you here?" Silence except for a faint echo, hardly noticeable. Louder, "Padre Pio, where are you?" This time the echo was more definite.

Nicola turned back to the altar. A ray of light was now streaming down from one of the stained glass windows, leading the friar's gaze directly to the base of the altar and to Pio's body.

"Padre Pio!" He ran to the prone priest, and then dropped to his hands and knees beside him. Pio was lying face down.

The friar put his hand on his shoulder to turn him. Nicola then hesitated momentarily. Something was wrong. The hand with which he was bracing himself on the normally cold floor was warm and wet. Pulling his hand out of the shadows and up to his face, he realized it was bloody. Casting his eyes to the floor, he observed the pool of blood to be quite large. Quickly turning the monk on his back, Nicola lifted him slightly and cradled him in his arms. "Pio, please answer me!"

Brother Nicola cried out for help, louder and louder until the other friars came running. "What is it? What has happened?" the Father Guardian asked, half out of breath.

"He's bleeding, unconscious. See how much blood! It's all over and he doesn't answer-but he still breathes."

Brother Ferdinando grabbed a candelabrum from the altar and began lighting the candles. As they began to illuminate the room and Pio, Brother Nicola gasped. "Look at Pio's face! It seems to have a glow about it!"

The others noticed it also. Pio's eyes were now open, but he gazed off toward the crucifix as if no one were there.

"Pio ... " begged Brother Nicola, still cradling him in his arms. He gave the monk a small shake. Pio's eyes slowly rolled over to meet Nicola's. "Pio ...It's me, Nicola. Let me carry you to your room, and we shall call for the doctor."

"No doctor!" Pio replied hoarsely. With these words he turned from Nicola's grip. He tried to raise himself up, but his hand slipped on the bloody floor, and he fell back.

"Let us help you," Brother Nicola said, moving toward the priest. But the bleeding man crawled away, out of the puddle toward a bench. There he pulled himself up and started for the door.

"Let us carry you!" **Brother Arcangelo** insisted as he grabbed his arm, but the injured monk struggled free of his grasp.

All at once the brothers knew not to interfere. All they could do was to follow the bloody trail he was leaving.

"He will bleed to death!" **Brother Ferdinando** exclaimed.

Before anyone could answer, Padre Pio was out the door into the corridor and onto the steps. He moved swiftly, leaning against the walls to maintain his balance. At the top of the stairs he turned and spoke into the stairwell, "Think of yourselves!" And again he turned and went along the passageway to cell number five, his own. A push on the door and he was inside, out of sight of the others.

"You wait here," said the Father Guardian to the gathered friars, "I will go into his cell and see what can be done. I will call if I need help." He entered, the door swung shut and no sound came forth.

Outside the closed door the five friars tried to pull all that had happened into perspective. "What do you know of all this, Nicola?" asked **Brother Carmelo**, a usually quiet but thoughtful friar.

"I saw nothing, heard nothing. I came by the door to the chapel and saw him at prayer. A few minutes later he was lying on the floor. I should have stayed closer. I…" Nicola fell silent, recalling the frightening sight and the emotion it had evoked.

"Do not blame yourself, Nicola. He has been sick for some time. Finding him a few minutes earlier certainly wouldn't have made much difference. He's still alive, praise be to God."

Nicola was not comforted by these words. "How long can he live?" He said excitedly, "You see the way he bleeds! Why hasn't anyone gone for the doctor? What are we thinking about, standing here like this? One of us should go for the doctor before ... "

The Father Guardian, who had just stepped out of the cell, interrupted him. "A doctor is not needed," he said in a soft-spoken voice. The Father Guardian had a blank expression on his face, as though he was drugged.

"Is he dead?" blurted Brother Nicola. "No ...He's alive."

"But he will bleed to death if we do not get a doctor!"

"He will not. He is in the care of God. He will live, I am sure.

"Today Jesus visited him in our chapel. Our Padre Pio bears **The Wounds of Christ…the stigmata**!"

The Father Guardian began to make his way down the narrow corridor, and made no motion to dismiss the friars. Nicola slowly went to his knees and began to pray. The others followed in reverent silence.

Chapter 3.

The doors of Saint Mary of Graces were kept open to all, but the entrance to the monastery was locked on that day, September 20, 1918, immediately after two of the friars left on errands of great import.

Brother Nicola was sent with tidings of the holy event to **Foggia**, where the **Provincial Father** resided. **Brother Gaudenzio** was dispatched on the much longer journey to **Pietrelcina**, Padre Pio's native village. Hopefully, **Don Salvatore Pannullo**, pastor of the local church and the priest whom Pio studied under, could lend credence to today's phenomena.

Chapter 4.

At the village, Brother Gaudenzio went directly to the church and introduced himself to Don Salvatore Pannullo. He gave a full accounting of the events of September 20. Rather than showing shock or dismay, Don Salvatore listened silently, giving an occasional sympathetic nod.

"I knew from the beginning that he was special. He was the best of my **chierichetti** ... the finest of my little dear ones. And now he must surely be a saint." The old archpriest became silent, contemplative. He removed his rimless bifocals and set them on the small table beside him. Brother Gaudenzio observed that Don Salvatore's eyes were watering.

Brother Gaudenzio broke the silence. "Have you known Pio always?"

The archpriest cleared his throat and began rubbing the bridge of his nose with his thumb and forefinger, self-consciously trying to hide his tears. Although in his late sixties, Gaudenzio observed, Don Salvatore had the trim physique of a man half his age. His sturdy frame and furrowed face made the tears look out of place.

Chapter 5.

"I baptized him the day after his birth, in the spring of 1887. His birth was uneventful, attended by the midwife, **Grazia Fromichelli**. He was the second of eight children born to his parents, **Orazio Forgione**, his papa, who was then about twenty-five, and **Maria Giuseppe de Nunzio Forgione**, who was about two years older. Both his parents had also been born right here in Pietrelcina. The midwife was his godmother. The family, like all others here about, lived in poverty. Their address then, as I remember, was number 25, **Vico Storto**, a one-room hovel.

"He was baptized **Francesco**. His *marna* chose the name. She always had a deep devotion to **St. Francis of Assisi**. Of the eight children born to Pio's parents, three died in infancy, so he now has a brother, **Michele,** and three sisters, **Felicita, Pellegrina,** and **Grazia.** Grazia has become a nun."

"Were there any peculiar signs in his younger years?" Brother Gaudenzio asked.

"Real signs later, those that were perhaps recognizable. But from the things I have been told by his mama and papa, and by Pio himself, he was graced by heaven as well as pursued by the devil at a very early age, in his infancy. I recall the time his mama came to me frightened and grieved. In a fit of anger, provoked by the infant Francesco, his father, Orazio, had thrown the baby to the floor. For months the infant had been waking in the night screaming and crying. Only if the parents would sit up with him would he be silent, and then only if a light were lit.

"After months of this Orazio lost all control and cursing grabbed up the infant and flung him to the floor. Happily, the child was not injured, but Orazio never forgave himself. Do not misunderstand; he was devoted to the child, and loved him deeply. It was an act of passion, and I now wonder if the man was not momentarily possessed." Don Salvatore Pannullo paused thoughtfully a moment, then continued.

"Years later Francesco confided to me that his fits of crying and screaming were brought on by visitations, nightmares of fierce animals, monsters, creatures-the same forms that the devil took in later years…" The archpriest paused again, "But that is another matter; I'm getting ahead of myself."

Don Salvatore offered his guest some wine, bread, and cheese and took some for himself. "Anyway, to answer your question, these things have been part of his life since the beginning. How would one suspect? It is not unusual for a child to cry the night through ... but then, what person recalls in later years what frightening dreams he had as an infant? I can't recall what I dreamed last night. But I doubt not a word that comes from the mouth of our friend."

The two men sipped from their glasses, each contemplating his own thoughts. "Were all his early experiences horrors?" Brother Gaudenzio asked.

"Ah, no. He told me that from the very beginning he was protected from those devil monsters by his guardian angel."

"When did he first tell you of the angel?"

"Strangely, not until he was in his early teens. When I asked him why he never mentioned such a glorious thing to me before, he looked surprised. He'd assumed that everyone had such a companion and that it was no more unusual than having parents, grandparents or siblings."

"Didn't you doubt the boy?"

"If so, not for long, certainly not long enough to remember it. After all, it is not unusual for a child to have an imagined playmate or companion. Perhaps that is how I first envisioned what he was telling me, but as we talked I sensed, and don't ask me why, that this was different. Even to this day, he calls his guardian angel 'the companion of my youth'. I think this explains why he didn't play much with other children. He always seemed to be happy alone. But when I would watch him he didn't seem so much as a child by himself. It wasn't as if he were alone with his thoughts and dreams. It was as if he shared his solitude with another…an invisible friend. It wasn't really something that was obvious ... yet it was more like something one could sense."

"Yes," the friar agreed, "It is still that way now."

Chapter 6.

Don Salvatore continued his story, "When Francesco was about five years old his parents moved the family out of number 25, which had been the Forgione home for four decades, to number 1, Vico Storto, just down the narrow street. It doubled the space to two rooms for the growing family. It also made available to little Francesco the **Morgia**. This was the name he affectionately gave to a small run-down, one room shack that sat on a huge rock. It had been some sort of animal shelter and still contained some old straw. It was difficult to enter and of no use to anyone. Little Francesco claimed it. It would become an important part of his holy life.

"As a child, in his preteen years, Francesco was more likely to be off by himself than with his playmates. He was always slight, thin, and easily prone to colds and lung infections. His health was a constant worry to his parents, especially his mother. In those days pneumonia was a constant threat to life, even more than today, and for those with weak lungs tuberculosis has always been a real danger.

"One of the real incongruities of Francesco's personality," Don Salvatore recalled, "was that, in spite of his frail stature, he enjoyed wrestling. He became quite good at the sport and enjoyed the test of strength." Salvatore smiled at the recollection. "Frail as he was, when he wrestled he had surprising strength. Boys much larger, heavier and apparently stronger than Francesco could not match his skill and strength when they competed. Yet he refused to fight anyone for any reason other than sport. I've seen boys taunt him, hit him, hurt him mercilessly ... boys who he could easily beat at sport, and he would not lift a finger against them."

"Perhaps he was saving that for his many bouts with the devil," Brother Gaudenzio suggested. "Perhaps."

Chapter 7

Don Domenico Tizzani was a defrocked priest who lived in Pietrelcina. If he was not an agent of the devil, he was at least an obstacle on Francesco's path to the pulpit. Gaining an education in the small village was difficult, especially for the poverty-stricken. The apostate priest did everything in his power to discourage Francesco's education.

Those townspeople who had had dealings with the man considered him a good teacher. That part of his reputation was not tarnished. The fact that he lived publicly with a concubine and daughter was another matter. Francesco had started his education with two literate farmers in the area. They taught only the basics of reading and writing. Francesco soon exhausted what they could teach and was recommended to Tizzani.

On the first day Francesco came late to his lesson. "Is this the way you intend to impress me?" Tizzani asked sarcastically.

"I am sorry, sir, I was late getting out of Mass this morning."

"If you seek wisdom, you'll have to choose between the church and me, young man."

"There is no choice in that case," Francesco answered candidly. From that moment on there was little hope that any productive relationship would ever develop between student and teacher. The two met together for several months.

Francesco had nothing but contempt for his tutor. He complained to his parents, "He is a sinner. He openly lives in sin in his home. He has turned his back on God."

In spite of Tissani's ravings against the church the boy continued to go to church both before and after his lessons, which seemed to infuriate the teacher. The friction between the two became so great that the youth could learn nothing.

"Your son has no aptitude for learning," Tizzani finally told Francesco's mother. "Better you send him to the fields and let him earn an honest wage."

"Stop his schooling? You can't be serious. His father has gone to America to earn enough money to educate him. He is a bright child. How can you tell me he has an empty head?"

She wrote of the situation to Orazio, and by return mail he instructed, "Find a new teacher. Francesco is to become a monk." The new teacher was **Angelo Caccavo**. He didn't mind how much time his pupil spent in church. He in fact encouraged him. The boy progressed rapidly. After two years Caccavo had to admit there was nothing more he could teach him.

Chapter 8

It was hot; unusual weather for so late in the fall. It had been an uncomfortable, humid sweltering night. Francesco had not slept well. But something other than the weather bothered him. A sensation, an awareness, a presence haunted him. In the midst of the heat there was a chill at the back of his neck. It had been there during the night. It stayed with the dawn. As he dressed, walked to church, sat down in the chapel he loved so deeply, as he prayed and as he received Holy Communion, it accompanied him. It brought to mind the nightmares he'd had as an infant and so often throughout his youth. It was there with him, and it was, he felt sure, *evil.*

"You look pale this morning," his mother had remarked when he arose from his bed. "Don't you feel well?"

"I feel well, Mother. It is nothing for worry. I just slept poorly. The heat. I will be fine. I must get to Mass." But he didn't feel fine, and he knew it was something other than that he slept restlessly. But what was it? Certainly nothing that he could explain to anyone. *Better that she doesn't worry. I shall ask my Guardian Angel.* But the angel would not appear.

Where are you my friend? Does this thing frighten you too? And then he realized that he too was frightened. *Something will happen today. I know it; I feel it. I feel so alone. There is something…someone here, but it is not for me. This thing opposes me. It hates me. It seeks to harm me, destroy me. Dear angel and companion, please help me to understand.*

There was only that other friendly presence.

He decided to remain after Mass and sit alone to meditate as he often did. As the church emptied, the presence became stronger. He looked about. *I am alone, but I know I'm not alone.* "Who, what, where are you?" he mouthed. "Let me see you! Show yourself! I know you are here, whoever, whatever you are. Show yourself!"

Suddenly Francesco became very cold. Yet he began to perspire profusely, but he was chilled to his bones. He ached and shivered with the cold, like a chill with a fever. *Maybe Mama was right. Maybe I am to be sick again.* He dreaded the thought of another illness of his lungs that had plagued him so often over the past few years. *No, this is not like that. It is different. I can tell a cold or lung attack. This is different. Something else is happening to me.* His fear and anxiety grew stronger. He felt threatened…desperate.

Now it became very bright ... a blinding light. The chill went away. The perspiration seemed to vanish. He was unaware of any feeling at all. No, that was not correct; he was acutely aware of having no physical sensation. *There is only the light…blue…white, I can't tell for sure…so very bright…only the light. I have no feeling, no sound, no taste, or smell. But wait, there is an odor, none that I have every experienced before. There is just the light, my thoughts, and that fragrance. I've never smelled anything like that before. Pleasant, but what is it?*

And now the light began to fade and Francesco found himself in a huge, magnificent hall, palatial, but not a palace of this world. On one side were a multitude of beautiful people, lovely people, sweet people, and mirrors, candles and tapestries of indescribable beauty. Francesco was in the midst of this hall, perhaps a ballroom. He turned to the other side and there he saw a rabble of hideous, grotesque creatures. Flame, smoke, horror seemed to consume that side of the vast room. He started to turn back, away from the vile creatures, but when he had spun around the beauty was replaced by a great cloud, and through it he could make out an approaching figure. Before he could see it clearly enough to make it out he knew it was that ... that something he had felt present in the night, that morning, in the church after Mass. And he feared it ... feared it as nothing he had ever feared before. Now he would have to face it. And he was afraid he would have to face it alone.

There was a tremendous roar, inhuman, ear shattering. A monstrous figure broke out of the cloud. A devil, straight out of the depths of hell, was coming at Francesco, determined to devour him.

At the last moment Francesco sensed that aroma again, and Jesus took him by his right arm. And His words filled the space, **"Francisco, that is the fiend against whom you will have to fight the rest of your days!"**

There was a flash, and a bolt of lightening struck the devil monster, and with a hideous scream it and *the vision drifted away.*

Chapter 9

Gena Mancuso was a beauty. She had striking red hair, unusual for that area of Pietrelcina. She was about a year younger than Francesco. When she'd been just twelve she was physically mature, appearing seventeen or eighteen. At that time a number of the older boys and several of the young men of the village had tried her, and most had succeeded. To say she was promiscuous was to be kind. Her smooth skin was dark but showed a bridge of freckles over her straight nose from each of her high-boned cheeks. She had piercing, bright, and sparkling eyes that danced in their deep-set sockets. They wavered between blue and green depending on how the light-struck at them. She was slim but not without noticeable curves. Her long legs accented her attractive figure, and when she walked with graceful strides she seemed to naturally flaunt all her physical assets.

With all of the men and boys of Pietrelcina scrambling after Gena, it was strange that she had an attraction for the scrawny, almost sickly Francesco.

"There goes your idol, Gena," a friend would say teasingly, as Franci walked by on his way to church, or to his Morgia, where he could be alone to meditate. "What is it you see in him? It'll take more than him to get you into heaven."

"Mind your own business. He's a really nice person. What's wrong if I just like someone because he's nice?"

"He doesn't even know we're alive. All he knows is church and books and praying."

"That's not true. He's good to talk to."

"Did you ever try anything but talk?" the friend asked, and Gena took a playful swing at him.

"It wouldn't even occur to me."

But that was not true. She'd thought it strange herself, that the deeper Francesco became involved with religion and the more he withdrew from his peers, the more she seemed to want him. Often her friends dared her to try to arouse Francesco to some act of lust, but she didn't want any part of that. She lusted for Francesco secretly, as if driven by some supernatural power. The more religious he became, the stronger her cravings grew. And though she had ambivalent feelings about it, she knew that some day she would try to have him, without her friends' knowledge.

Gena began having strange dreams. They were always the same. The recurring dream was a nightmare, but it didn't frighten her. She even looked forward to bedtime so that she might have the dream again. Beating of what sounded like kettledrums heralded each time the dream would come. It was a slow, monotonous beat, like the rhythm used on a galley ship to keep the slaves rowing in cadence.

"Gena, Gena, it is I, keeper of your soul," a deep, gruff voice would call. "My lovely Gena, you are so beautiful, and you must use your beauty for me." Now a face would appear with the voice, not a human face, it was grotesque but somehow attractive to her. Slowly after the face a body materialized, muscular, huge, hair-covered, masculine, unclad. It was not the body of a man, but manlike, and to Gena very erotic. The creature came continuously closer, and Gena realized that she was the one moving ... floating toward the nocturnal visitor. "You will do my bidding, Gena. I will grant you great favor, teach you great pleasure, all if you only serve me." There was a hypnotic quality to the words. She felt her will being possessed. At first she wanted to resist the creature, but as he spoke to her she wanted more and more to resign herself to him.

The dream became more vivid. She felt herself sinking into a mass of silken pillows, a cool breeze stroking her gently, and the creature speaking constantly, the gruff voice mellowing, softening. Always at this point in each of the dreams Gena discovered herself desiring the creature, hungering with her body for his embrace. "You were created for love, Gena, you are capable of so much love, Gena. You will give yourself to me and for me. Give your body, give your love." With those words the creature mounted but never penetrated. But just the presence, the embrace caused Gena a pleasure and satisfaction she's never known in the waking world. "I promise you pleasures far greater than that, Gena. Pleasure beyond any you've ever dreamed of will be yours when you serve me, dearest Gena."

Now the creature begins to fade and drift away, but the voice is still clear, "Gena, the young Francesco, he must be yours. He is the key to your greatest pleasures."

Chapter 10

Brother Camillo was a Capuchin friar who lived in the Pietrelcina area while Francesco was young. He was a great influence on the boy. Francesco loved everything about the friar, his brown robe with its white cord for a belt, the unique hood, for which the Capuchins were named, but most of all the little beards the Capuchins were known for. Other monks and priests were usually smooth-shaven. The Capuchins as a group were bearded.

Furthermore, Francesco wanted to be a friar-priest rather than a monk-priest. Monks were assigned and restricted to their religious house or monastery for life. Friars had considerably more freedom and could work more with the people. Friars considered themselves a brotherhood rather than a monastic order, and that appealed to Francesco. This distinction, his love for Brother Camillo, and the little beards made him determined to become a Capuchin ... even though other disciplines would have been easier.

The Capuchins are one of three branches of the Franciscans. They were established in the year 1528, in Italy. Their purpose was to return to the original interpretation of the Rule as written in 1209 by St. Francis of Assisi, Francesco's namesake.

Francesco's papa had returned to the United States of America, as he had done several times before, to earn a living for his family and to provide money for the boy's education. He spent periods of a year or two working at hard labor and construction, as did many of the men of Pietrelcina. In that poverty-stricken Italian village, even the low wage paid foreign laborers in America was a fortune. This money made it possible for the family to move from the one-room hovel at number 25 to the two-room structure at number 1. That hard-earned money and sacrifice give Francesco his needed education to qualify for entry into the **Capuchin friary at Morcone.**

Shortly before Francesco was to leave for Morcone and his new life he made one of his usual visits to his Morgia. Once inside, he knelt to pray, as usual, and to pass time with his Guardian Angel. Then he realized he was not alone. There was a sound from the dark corner behind him. "Who is there?" he asked as he turned to see. He squinted to see into the darkness.

"I've been waiting for you, Franci."

He immediately recognized the voice. "Gena, what are you doing here?"

"Don't be mad at me, Franci. I've watched you come here so often, I thought maybe we could talk."

"Why should I be mad at you, Gena? I would be happy to talk to you anytime you like. You've always been kind to me."

"Then it's alright that I come here to your…your special place?"

"Anyone can come here, Gena. It's just that no one does, so I came here when I want to meditate or pray."

"Why don't you pray in church?"

"I do," Francesco answered as he stood up, brushing straw from his knees. "But sometimes I just like to have even more solitude than in the church. Haven't you a private place, someplace you love more than any other, a place you consider all your own, a special place?"

"No ...but wait, yes, I did. When I was younger, a little girl, I did have. There was a small grove of trees in a corner of a field behind our house. There were thick bushes among them. I was small, and there was a space, like a narrow path, through which I could pass into the midst of that grove." A smile spread over her lovely face as she remembered. A sparkle emitted form her eyes. "I imagined that I was the only person alive who knew of that path and the small clearing in that grove. Maybe I was. You're the only person I've ever mentioned that grove to." Gena paused a moment. There was a small tear forming in the corner of her eye.

"It's a beautiful place, Gena."

"What do you mean? How could you?" Gena stopped in the middle of her question. There was a strangeness about Francesco. He was perfectly motionless, expressionless, as if his body were just an empty shell and the person inside absent. Then in another moment he was back, and he continued to speak.

"It is nice and shady. The trees are evergreens and there is a carpet of pine needles on the ground. It is a small clearing. You'd barely get in there now. The little path is overgrown. It's been a long time since anyone's been here."

Gena stood dumbfounded. The glazed look about his eyes disappeared and he was fully returned. "Where was it you lived then, before you moved with your parents here to Pietrelcina?"

"We lived in the mountains north of here." Gena answered with an expression of disbelief still on her face. "But how did you know?"

Francesco answered matter-of-factly, "I just saw the place. I can't explain it. Did I describe it correctly?"

"Exactly!" Gena replied, still not wanting to believe what she had just heard. "It was exactly as you described. But how ... how is it possible?"

"I tell you, I can't explain it. It is just one of many things ... many things I can't explain." The boy shrugged his shoulders and smiled.

"Francesco, doesn't it frighten you?"

"No. These things came upon me slowly. Gradually. And I became used to them. I keep them to myself. Others would think me mad if…"

Gena interrupted, "What other things?"

Francesco hesitated only a few seconds, then answered, "Well, I sometimes know things before they happen. For instance, a few weeks ago I walked by a place in the road that crosses the fields just outside the village. I stopped at the spot because I heard bells ringing, beautiful chimes. No one else heard them. Don Salvatore was there. I told him that a beautiful new church would be built on that exact spot. It will be, too. A long time will pass yet, but it will be built there, I have no doubt."

Francisco could see the doubt in Gena's eyes. "Gena, I also know why you are here today."

"What do you mean?" Terror was stamped in her expression. "You are here to do the devil's bidding, Gena."

The expression of terror changed to anger. Her usually calm, beautiful eyes showed hate and appeared to contain fire. And when she spoke again it was not with her voice. It was gruff, loud, deep, the voice that visited her almost nightly now. "Your soul be damned, Francesco Forgione, you can't trifle with me. You can't ignore me." And she lunged at Francesco screaming profanities, swinging her fists, kicking.

Francesco stood his ground and deflected her blows. "It is not you, Gena. I know this is not you. The devil has hidden himself in you. He cannot fool me. I hold no ill will toward you, Gena." And as he uttered those words she turned and ran out the opening in the shack that served as a door. Francesco knelt down once more on the straw-covered floor and gave thanks for the courage and protection heaven had sent.

Chapter 11

On January 22, 1903, while he was still fifteen, Francesco was invested as a novice into the Capuchin friary at Morcone, Italy. He received a habit: robe, white cord belt, and sandals. He also took the name Pio, honoring Pope Pius V. Until his ordination into the priesthood, he would answer to Fra Pio. He was not yet under obligation to remain in the order. He dressed himself in his new garments and started growing his Capuchin beard.

The following year he made his first vows to live for three years in poverty, chastity, and obedience to the **Rule of St. Francis of Assisi**. During these three years he studied for the priesthood, majoring in philosophy.

Chapter 12

Shortly after he took his first vows, Fra Pio took ill. It started as one of his bouts with bronchitis, but this time he ran fever continuously for several days. He refused to eat. He was willing to drink only water and the juice from lemons. He lapsed in and out of delirium. The doctor was called and prescribed bed rest, fluids, and sponging when the fever rose above 103 degrees Fahrenheit. "If ever the fever does not come down after half an hour of sponging, send for me."

On the sixth night of Fra Pio's illness, an excited classmate of the patient knocked on the doctor's door, rousing him from sleep. "What is it?" and realizing it was one of the seminary students, "Is it Fra Pio? His fever?"

"Yes, you must come quickly, doctor. We've sponged as you directed, but the fever rises fearfully. He is thrashing and delirious. We cannot hold him. He is so hot it hurts to touch him ... like hot dishwater!"

"How high is the fever?"

"We cannot measure it any more."

"I don't understand. Surely you can hold him still long enough to take the temperature."

"Just barely, Doctor. But our thermometer does not measure high enough."

With that, the doctor wasted not another second at talk but pulled on his coat over his pajamas, grabbed his bag, and ran with the student back to the friary.

Arriving at Fra Pio's room the physician took a few moments to recover his breath and then examined the patient. His first words were: "This is not possible. This fever is incompatible with life. Start sponging-quickly!"

They sponged under the doctor's supervision, but the fever refused to drop. It was not measurable on the doctor's thermometer. To touch Fra Pio's skin was like putting one's hand in hot bath water. It was tolerable, but at first touch it was painful enough to make one want to withdraw.

"Bring me a kitchen thermometer," the physician demanded. In a minute one of the students returned with the implement.

"Good, this will measure his fever," the doctor said, taking the large thermometer and placing it under Fra Pio's arm at the shoulder. Three students held Fra Pio to the bed so he could not break the glass device while thrashing.

The doctor measured the time with a pocket watch he borrowed, having left his own at home with his clothes. "Three minutes!" and he took the thermometer from under Fra Pio's arm. The students were relieved to be able to relinquish their hold on their sick brother.

"This is impossible!" the physician exclaimed in disbelief.

"It must be in error." He looked again at the thermometer and back to the thrashing friar. "This measures 125 degrees. It is absolutely impossible! This thermometer must be wrong. It just cannot be."

"Would a garden thermometer work, Doctor?" one of the students asked.

"Yes, it would be a check. Get it if you have one." It too registered 125 degrees.

The doctor spent the rest of the night at Fra Pio's bedside, knowing that the young friar would not survive the night. Such a high fever would kill him momentarily. By all medical rules he should have died anytime after the fever climbed past 106 degrees to its present level. "Even if his temperature were to come down now his brain will be damaged from the heat. He or it cannot survive this fever."

Fra Pio continued thrashing deliriously, mumbling and screaming. They tried to protect him from injuring himself, from falling off his cot. If death were in that room that night, it kept its distance from Fra Pio. Just before dawn the doctor confessed, "If I hadn't been here to see this I'd not have believed it, no matter who would have told it to me." He paused a moment, then added, "My colleagues will never believe me."

Then, just as the dawn broke, Fra Pio's thrashing and delirium stopped. He had a calm about him that had not been there for days. The doctor noticed and went to his side, expecting the end was at hand. He felt for a pulse and was surprised to find it strong and slow normal. More surprising was that the fever was down. In fact, as the physician held the patient's hand, he could feel the temperature drop.

The friar opened his eyes, looked at the astonished physician and said, "Good morning, Doctor." He looked about the room at the friars who had been keeping the vigil with the doctor. "Good morning, Brothers. We must hurry, else we'll be late for Mass."

After Mass, which Fra Pio insisted on attending against the doctor's advice, the physician re-examined his patient. He was completely recovered. "Do you realize how sick you were, how close to death, Fra Pio?" the doctor asked.

"I have not been that ill, Doctor. It's only the fire which burns in my heart." He said no more. He got up and left the room to return to his studies. Bewildered the doctor repeated, " My collogues will never believe me." And they didn't...at least not yet.

Chapter 13

"I, Fra Pio, vow and promise to almighty God, to the Blessed Virgin Mary, to our holy Father St. Francis, to all the saints, and to you, Father, to observe all the days of my life, the **Role of the Friars Minor**, confirmed by **Pope Honorius**, living in obedience, without property, and in chastity." These are the words that Fra Pio swore in 1907. Having professed these final vows, he moved to **the house of studies at San Marco Ia Catola**.

On August 10, 1910, **Frate Pio of Pietrelcina** was ordained priest, at the **Cathedral of Benevento**. In the presence of his mother, brother and sisters, and the archpriest of Pietrelcina, Don Salvatore, Fra Pio became **Padre Pio**. Immediately after his ordination, at the age of twenty-three, Padre Pio said his first Mass in that cathedral. The only sadness of that day was that his father, Orazio, could not be there. He was still in America, laboring to make it all possible.

Chapter 14

During the seven years from the time that Francesco donned the robes of a Franciscan novice to the day he was ordained a Capuchin friar-priest, little changed in Pietrelcina.

Gena never forgot her experience in the Morgia. Her nightly visitations stopped. Two years later she married. She never spoke of the incident with anyone. Her longing for the scrawny, religious boy eased and then completely disappeared. She remained a beauty, even after the three children she bore, and everyone in Pietrelcina agreed that she was a good mother and wife despite her beginnings.

The entire village had followed Padre Pio's progress while he had been a student. When he was ordained, the entire community took pride, and Don Salvatore suggested several times that Padre Pio should consider taking the pulpit in his native village. Padre Pio declined.

As proud as the villagers were of their seminarian, so were they concerned for him when they heard of his increasingly severe illnesses. They worried about his high fevers and weight losses. And when they heard of his sudden recoveries they knew it to be the work of God,… a miracle. There were the skeptics who were convinced that the sicknesses were exaggerated or that they were the symptoms of a hysterical religious fanatic. But the second time, and each succeeding time after that, when the fevers came, the doctor took one or another colleague with him to examine the student friar. Regardless of how much the consultants doubted when they came to the bedside, they were convinced by the time they left. Even if those fevers were artificially induced, the high temperatures for such long periods would kill the man, or at least do irreversible damage to him, to anyone, both physically and mentally. In each case, as in the first, recovery was sudden and complete.

༄ ༄ ༄ ༄

Gena had a dream. It was a cool night. Gena, in her sleep, began to perspire and toss, and then she became calm and went into a very deep sleep. Had anyone tried to rouse her at that moment they'd have thought her in a coma. She dreamed a great gray cloud approached her. Again, she heard the drums and then a familiar voice out of the past.

"Gena, my sweet, beautiful Gena. Come to me, Gena." This time the dream was different in that Gena spoke to the voice for the first time in their many encounters. She spoke in pleading tones, "Please, I know you, I tried. Please, don't harm me. Please leave me. I can't help you."

"Gena, we are friends. You needn't fear me. I mean you no harm. I've never brought you anything but pleasure, great pleasure, wonderful pleasures."

There was that hypnotic quality again. Gena felt her will slipping from her. "Gena, you tried. You did as well as you could. Failure was not your fault." Now the figure appeared out of the cloud. He was as before. "You did all you could, Gena. The next time you will succeed. You will not fail me, Gena. You will pleasure with the priest."

"Please, I cannot. I am faithful. My family, I can't…"

"Gena, you can. You will. I command you. You will; you want to." Again she drifted to him. She felt herself on the familiar pillows, the familiar comfort. She knew what would come next. She wanted it to happen.

"Gena, you cannot resist my pleasures."

He came to her, embraced her. She could feel the passion rush through her body. She pressed herself against him, clutched at him. "Take from me, Gena. Take all the pleasure you want." And for the first time she felt him penetrate her. The pleasure was deep, full, instantaneous. Every muscle tightened about him and then suddenly released, tightened and released, again and again. She clutched at him and screamed with pleasure.

"I will return to you, Gena."

She awoke with her orgasmic scream.

"What is it, Gena, my dear, what is it?" her startled husband exclaimed, shaking her.

"Oh, what? Oh, I'm sorry. I just had a dream. A frightening dream."

"Are you alright now?" He tried to comfort her, put his arm around her.

"I'm alright. I'm sorry I woke you. I'll be fine. Go back to sleep," and she pulled away from him, her thoughts on a priest she hardly knew anymore, but for whom she was lusting.

Chapter 15

Most of Pietrelcina talked of Padre Pio's return. Most just looked forward to seeing an old friend. Many joined to consider how they could best interest him in staying to assist their aging archpriest, Don Salvatore. And there were the skeptics, those who doubted all the stories that had filtered back to the village about the Capuchin.

"These are exaggerations, imagination…"

"I have wild dreams too. If I were a priest, you'd call them visions also…"

"Believe me, God doesn't need the help of one of us to fight the devil…"

"I remember him when he was just a kid. I thought he was mad then; now I know I was right. I talk to myself, too. Does that make me special?"

It would not be long after Padre Pio's return to the village that the people would have plenty to talk about. The skeptics would have to think twice. Those who believed would never have to fear doubting in the future. None would openly laugh about the man ever again.

Padre Pio came home obviously ill. He had to be helped from the wagon that brought him from San Marco la Cataula. The word quickly spread from those who saw him come into the village.

"Our Padre Pio is here. I fear he has come home to die. He looks to have both feet in the grave already…"

"There is no hope for the man. He has surely said his last Mass…"

"He asked to be taken first to the old shack. You know, the one he always went into as a boy. The wagon man had to help him in. Then he came out and drove his wagon off. Padre Pio is still in there. He might be dead already. Maybe someone should go to see…"

After 45 minutes people started to gather in the road near the Morgia.

"Did you see him when he went in? He looked half dead. Had to be carried in."

"It was terrible. I'm so sad for him. I'm sure he's gone to say his final prayer."

"Perhaps we should go see about him."

"Do we dare? Wouldn't he call if he needed help?"

"He didn't look to have the strength left to call for help. He's come home to die.

"I think we should… "

A hush fell on the group. They were dumbstruck as they looked at the entrance to the Morgia. Padre Pio walked out of the opening, a bright smile on his face at the sight of his friends gathered in the road to meet him. He strode toward them, straight and robust. He was completely changed from when he had entered the old shack. People who saw him come into town on the wagon would swear for the rest of their days that it was a miracle. Some of those who saw neither his entrance into town nor his exit from the Morgia just had more to be skeptical about. But this was just the beginning of the strange events that would take place in Pietrelcina over the next few years.

Padre Pio made no fuss over his recovery in the Morgia. He was used to such phenomena. "I am not concerned with the state of my health anymore. You must not be concerned either. I must concern myself only with my soul and my spiritual being. Concern yourselves not about me, my dear friends; think only to do God's will."

Then he went straight to his mother's house and ate as he had not eaten in weeks, pasta and tomato sauce, enough to feed an army of priests. From there he went to the church, **Saint Mary of the Angels**, to see his friend, the archpriest Don Salvatore Pannullo.

"Padre Pio, how wonderful to see you again, but you look so wonderful. I've expected an invalid from the reports that preceded you. Well, I'm glad you're here and looking so well. Tell me when you're ready and I'll put you to work."

"My dear friend, I am ready."

The next day Padre Pio was saying Mass in the church that he had come to love as a child, Saint Mary of the Angels. The villagers were shocked when his Mass lasted three hours. Pio seemed to slip into a celebration all his own, and lose all track of time. He would stand motionless for as long as thirty minutes during certain prayers at the altar, even though these prayers were only a few short paragraphs in length. So genuine was his communion, his piety, that the villagers didn't notice the time pass during the service. They were mesmerized. Those who didn't attend talked about the "crazy monk" who gave a three-hour Mass. Those who took part in the Mass did not mind its length, but it was incompatible with their hard work schedules. Don Salvatore had to call this to Padre Pio's attention. After that, only his Sunday Mass took so long, and every bench was filled.

Chapter 16

All his siblings had moved out of the little home at number I, Vico Storto. Orazio, Pio's father, had gone back to America after a short visit home. His mother Giuseppe insisted that Pio take the one bedroom for himself. She would occupy and sleep in the other room, which served as the kitchen-living room. Pio argued, but she would have it no other way.

Padre Pio maintained his habit of getting up at two in the morning to start his Morning Prayer and meditation, so he retired early. As soon as the sun went down he would withdraw to his little bed chamber, close the wooden shutter inside the window, say his final prayers for the day, and go to bed.

He had only been back to town for a week when he began to fast again, receiving nothing except Holy Communion for his nourishment. And the low-grade fevers began to return. He became withdrawn and spent more and more time at his Morgia.

He continued his fast into a second week, and his behavior became increasingly strange. His day consisted of saying Mass in the mornings and spending the entire remainder of the day on his knees in the little structure until it was time to retire to his bed at night. His mother became worried, but didn't know how to handle the situation. Pio had withdrawn from her also. There was little conversation between the mother and her son. She was tempted to talk to Don Salvatore, but had reservations about interfering.

At 10 o'clock in the night of August 14th, Giuseppe was awakened from a sound sleep by a loud banging. *Someone's pounding on my door.... Who can it be at this late hour?* The thundering banging continued. "One moment, please!" she yelled as she tied the string of her robe. The noise didn't stop. Has something happened to my Orazio in America? Her annoyance turned into anxiety. She rushed to the front door but stopped just short of it. The pounding intensified, filling the room. The noise wasn't coming from the front door. It was coming from the door to Pio's room.

She jumped as a vase sitting on a small shelf attached to the outer wall of Pio's room crashed to the floor. Then she noticed that the wall, which separated his room from the other, was trembling, as though an earthquake was in progress. But it was only his wall that shook.

"Pio!" She stood only inches away from his door, but dared not touch it. The terrible noise mounted, and she covered her ears with her hands. A few chips of plaster fell before her feet, and she sprang backwards. A cracking noise, and the plaster around the door jambs began breaking up like thin, sun-baked clay.

She couldn't stand it any longer. Her motherly instincts overpowered her fear. "Francesco! Please, let me in!" She was trying to open the door, but it wouldn't budge. Clinching her fists, she began hammering the door.

"Francesco!" Her voice echoed in the room. The terrorizing banging had stopped. The little home stood silent. Padre Pio opened the door and stepped out into the light. Blood was dripping from the corner of his mouth.

Giuseppe was trembling. Tears rolled down her cheeks. Pio was deeply grieved to see his mama so upset. He came forward and put his arms around her. He held her tight while condemning himself for bringing such pain to one he loved so much.

"Francesco ... The door would not open ... I tried, but..."

"Hush, Mama… I bolted the door myself. No harm will ever come to you, Mama. It is only my poor soul they are after."

"Who is after you?" she sobbed. "Your door ... the banging ... and the walls of your room. They were shaking!"

Pio put his hands on Giuseppe's small shoulders and gently broke their embrace. She looked up at him. His expression had become very solemn. "Mama," he began, "you can never come into my room when I'm in there. Do you understand?" Pio could see questions flashing in her eyes. "Please promise me this, Mama."

"My son, you can get help. Maybe Don Salvatore will be able…"

"NO!" Giuseppe was startled to hear Pio raise his voice. She had never heard him raise it before, not even as a young boy. He was always so quiet. "I'm sorry momma, I didn't mean to shout. This is my battle. No one can help. Please, Mama. Please understand."

Giuseppe lowered her head, and then gave a slight nod. Over the past weeks Pio had withdrawn from her. If she did not yield to his pleas, she was certain he would withdraw further-maybe even leave home. And she didn't want this to happen. *If only Orazio were here, maybe he could help our son.*

Pio bid his mother goodnight and went back to his room. The door swung shut, and she heard him bolt it from the other side. The remainder of the night remained calm, but she did not sleep well.

For the next three nights the same horrors continued. They would start precisely at 10 o'clock, and last twenty to thirty minutes. Giuseppe remained in her bed and said the rosary. But on the fifth night things became worse. The duration of the ordeal lasted well over an hour and a half. And there were voices. Many voices. And a stale stench emanated from Pio's door and walls. Giuseppe could withstand the knockings on the walls and door, but not the voices. She knew that they were from the depths of hell, and the thought of her son confronting these forces sent a chill through her flesh. She would talk with Don Salvatore in the morning.

Chapter 17

The old archpriest listened with deep concern. He had noticed Pio limping during the morning Mass. He also displayed pain when he moved his neck, back, and shoulders. It was difficult for him to raise his left arm above his shoulder, and there was a bruise on the left side of his face just in front of his ear, on the upper part of his cheekbone. Don Salvatore didn't mention this to the already alarmed Giuseppe.

"You say these noises occur around 10 p.m.?"

"Yes, Father. I dread the hour. Please, do something. I fear for my son's life!"

"What time does Padre Pio retire to his room?"

"He comes into the house and straight to his room a little after nine."

"I will be at your house at 8:45, Giuseppe. I'm sure we can put a stop to all this nonsense."

"Thank you, Father. Thank you." Relief was written all over her face. She turned and started down the walkway toward home. She held her head high and proud that she had done the right thing.

The archpriest stood on the porch and watched her as she disappeared in the distance. He had no idea what to expect that evening. Surely her descriptions of the previous nights were highly exaggerated, but there was enough sincerity and fright in her voice to indicate that there was something abnormal taking place at number 1, Vico Storto, and tonight would tell.

Don Salvatore arrived at Pio's home at 8:45 sharp. He paused at the door. If the incidences were half as horrible as Giuseppe had described them, what would he do? The only thing he knew of such phenomena was that which he had read about in his studies many long years ago. The stories were unbelievable, yet had actually been documented by the Church. The archpriest knocked on the door. Maybe nothing will happen.

"Please come in, Father." Giuseppe was smiling, but she looked very nervous. "May I get you some wine?"

"Thank you, no." Looking over to the corner he recognized one of his parishioners, **Gemma Vitalli**, sitting at the dinner table.

"Good evening, Father." Gemma giggled.

He gave her a small nod. What is she doing here? Is this some sort of picnic? The archpriest liked to believe that he had love for all his flock, but Gemma was one of a few he loved the least. She was the village's most notorious gossip, and Don Salvatore secretly thought of her as "Old Ratchet Jaw." Ratchet Jaw was in her early forties, he guessed, but tried to act much younger. Unlike most of the women in Pietrelcina, who were slim and sun-browned from working in the fields, she was overweight and had hardly any color in her face. Ratchet Jaw spent most of her time at home, either cooking or eating. Her husband, **Reggiani**, had passed away several years earlier, and had left behind over 200 acres of rich farmland. She in turn had rented five forty-acre parcels to different families for farming purposes. The income she received did not make her rich, but it did allow her to live comfortably.

Probably what Don Salvatore disliked most was having her in the confessional.

She could talk so long about nothing. "Bless me Father for I have sinned. My last confession was one week ago. Oh Father, I just don't know what to do. Someone's been sneaking around my home at night and peeping in my windows. I can feel their eyes on me as I'm dressing for bed. I'd call the constable but I've never been able to see the culprits face. But I know he's there. And I curse whoever it is. Cursing is a sin against God, and I feel so terribly guilty afterwards, but I just am not able to control myself. My neighbor…I'm sure you know who she is…tells me I should replace the lovely sheer curtains, which I have on my windows now with dark or heavy woven ones. But I like my sheers ... I just think that she's jealous because she can't afford them. And after all, why should I have to give up something because of what someone else is doing wrong? Don't you think the…"

Giuseppe spoke, pulling the archpriest from his thoughts.

"Gemma has brought me one of her delicious rhubarb pies. Would you ... er ... like a piece, Father?"

Don Salvatore sensed Giuseppe's embarrassment. Gemma had undoubtedly called unexpectedly, placing Giuseppe in a very awkward position.

"A slice of pie sounds very tempting, but a tooth with a small hole in it has been saying 'no' to sweets these past few days." *God will forgive me for this one little lie.*

Giuseppe turned to Gemma. "Gemma, would you like a slice?"

"Just a tiny one." She giggled again.

Giuseppe had not expected her to accept. She only made the offer out of politeness. But it had been done. *I wonder if her giggling bothers the Father as it does me…*

Don Salvatore surveyed the room. His eyes stopped at the door to Pio's chamber. The plaster was broken away from the doorjambs, the same as she had described it. Gemma was chattering in the background. He was paying no attention to the topic. *How does Giuseppe put up with that endless giggling?* He approached the door. I cannot show any signs of fear. He knew Giuseppe's eyes were watching him. *God give me strength.* He slowly pushed the door open, trying to act nonchalant so that he would not make Ratchet Jaw suspicious. The light from the main room cast his shadow on the floor before him. Straining his eyes, he spotted a candle atop a small table situated against the far wall. As he stepped forward, he tripped over a small object on the floor, but quickly regained his balance. Choosing his steps more carefully, he discovered the floor was heavily littered. *I would have never guessed him the untidy sort.* He lit the candle and picked it up. Turning around, he was shocked to see that the room was in complete shambles.

The books Pio loved so dearly were strewn about the floor. The bed was turned over, its mattress lying on the floor next to it. There were some bloodstains on the sheet. A small table was upturned, its armless wooden chair broken in the opposite corner of the room. A crucifix hung on the wall, askew. Flowers lay wilting beside a broken vase. One wall was splattered with ink. At its base a quill and broken well lay on the floor. *Could this be Pio's doing? Maybe his fevers make him delirious. There is nothing supernatural about a mess like this.* He thought about the broken plaster that surrounded the outer side of the door. He held the light close to the wall, which neighbored the inner side of the door.

Then he saw them. They were deeply engraved in the wall. Claw marks. There was no doubt. No human could have made such deep-seated imprints. He held the candle near the wall as he walked around the room. The marks were everywhere.

"What a terrible mess!" Gemma was standing in the doorway, her eyes bug-eyed at the sight before her. Giuseppe was standing directly behind her. Apparently Gemma was being led to the front door when she caught a glimpse of Pio's chambers. "What is that you're looking at, Father?" Gemma said as she began to take a step forward.

Giuseppe reached and lightly grasped Gamma's arm. Gemma paid no attention. She effortlessly pulled free and proceeded ahead. Giuseppe followed closely behind.

"This is nothing that concerns you, Gemma." The archpriest had an irritated tone in his voice.

"But I just thought that maybe…" Gamma's voice trailed off. Her eyes were riveted to the markings on the wall. "Oh dear God! What type of animal has done this? What do you keep in here, Giuseppe?"

Giuseppe looked at the wall, and then at Don Salvatore. Her eyes were filled with questions. He stared back at her blankly; he had no answers.

Gemma had stopped her babbling, drawing the attention of the other two occupants of the room. She stood motionless, apprehensive. She had sensed something. The archpriest now sensed it, too. There was another presence. No, there were many other presences. Cynical presences. Mocking laughter, which couldn't be heard by the ear. But it was there.

Gemma broke her silence. "It's cold in here, very cold. It's this room. Something is wrong in this room…" She wasn't talking with the normal giddiness in her voice. She spoke in a soft, slow, and composed tone, as if in a hypnotic state.

A horrible odor, like that of decayed flesh began to sting Don Salvatore's nostrils. He removed his handkerchief from his back pocket and covered his nose and mouth. "There is nothing more to see here," he said. "Let's go to the other room."

Giuseppe didn't hesitate at his suggestion, and rushed from the room, gagging. Gemma still remained motionless, and the archpriest had to take her arm and lead her out. He closed the door behind him. *I never want to go in there again. I feel so powerless!* At that moment, the front door swung open. It was Pio.

He glanced at Gemma. She was staring at him with wide, fearful eyes. Something had upset her. Then he looked over to his mother. A guilty look was written on her face. She put her head down for a moment before looking back up at Pio. His eyes were forgiving.

Don Salvatore approached the young priest. Putting his hand on Pio's shoulder, he began speaking in a voice barely louder than a whisper. "Padre Pio… What goes on here?"

"It is my battle." Pio was staring down at the floor in front of him, trying to avoid looking the archpriest directly in the face.

"There is evil in your room… It is no wonder you get so sick. I have never felt such a piercing cold!"

"In a short while, I will feel the fires of hell," Pio murmured.

"Padre Pio! What fate has God given you? Tonight I will stay with you. Maybe with two of us facing the... "

"No!" Pio straightened up and grasped Don Salvatore's hands. "Absolutely not! I will not allow it!"

The door to Pio's chambers burst open. "COME, HOLY ONE! YOU ARE KEEPING US WAITING!" Again the cynical laughter was sensed.

Gemma screamed and ran out of the house. Giuseppe stood motionless, petrified. Don Salvatore turned his head to Pio's

room, from which the voice had roared. Straining his eyes, he saw nothing.

"Padre Pio, I insist that you allow me to offer prayers with

you tonight. I am sure that..."

"Please! For the sake of the salvation of your soul, I beg that you leave this moment!" Pio was squeezing the archpriest's hands very tightly, like a small child pleading with his mother for a favor.

"And your mother, Padre...what is to become of her?"

"She is safe ... Tomorrow I will move to my Morgia. No longer will she have to share the torment, which is meant for me."

"Why must you face this thing alone, Padre?" Don Salvatore was unnerved by the evening's events, but his sincere concern for Pio's safety overshadowed his own fears.

"I do not face it completely alone, Father. I am not that strong. My guardian angel helps me, and He helps me."

"Very well. May God grant you the strength of the Angel Michael. Good night."

Pio nodded, entered his chamber, and closed the door behind him. All was silent. Don Salvatore went over to Giuseppe's side. "I believe that no mortal can lift the burden from your son, Giuseppe. But I am convinced that he walks with God. This explains why he is such a powerful enemy of Satan. Tomorrow he will move from this house."

Giuseppe put her head up high. "I will not allow him to leave. He told me I am safe. He has never lied to me. What a terrible mother I would be, deserting him because of a little smoke, when he is engulfed in the flames! No. He will stay here. Thank you for your help, Father."

"I have done nothing. I wish I could. Never in my life have I wished so hard for something." Don Salvatore walked to the front door. So far, all was quiet. "I must go now, Giuseppe. I must go and speak with Gemma. Word of this is not to get out. Good night."

Gemma lived only six houses down from Giuseppe's home. The archpriest knocked on her door for several minutes to no avail. He called out her name. Her next-door neighbor, Tina, heard the noise and came out onto her small porch. "Is that you, Father?" she called. "Gemma is not home. She left here a few minutes ago, but I think she went to see a friend. Is it true what she says happened at Padre Pio's home, the loud voices and the…"

It was too late. Ratchet Jaw was on the loose.

Chapter 18

Early the next morning, by dawn, a crowd had begun gathering in front of number 1, Vico Storto. Padre Pio had already arisen and was long since at the church of Saint Mary of the Angels, at prayer. The hushed talk of the gathering villagers awoke Giuseppe, who was unable to fall asleep until she saw her son leave his room for church that morning. She slipped on her clothes and opened the outer door to see what the stir was.

"Is Padre Pio all right?" came from the crowd. "We are all concerned. Is he well?"

"He is already at the church this morning," Giuseppe answered. "Thank you for your concern. He is well."

Then the curious crowd started to question, "What happened last night?"

"Yes, is there anything to see?"

"Is it true about the claw marks on the wall?"

"What about the voices?"

"What did he say happened?"

Giuseppe looked at her fellow villagers. Then she made her decision. "I am sorry. I can tell you nothing. I have work to do now, and I must say good-bye." She turned and shut the door.

The crowd wasn't satisfied, and headed off to see the archpriest. When they began asking him the same questions, he became very short with them. "I don't know what you have been told, but it is none of your concern. Why must you pry into something, which, I promise, will have no effect on you? Doesn't Padre Pio have enough trouble with his health without your trying to make him seem like some sort of spectacle? Go back to your work. I'll hear no more from you!"

During the months that followed, there was more talk about the encounters occurring between Pio and his adversaries. They were now occurring without frequency, about every third week, but always at night, always terrifying to hear. After a while, the villagers avoided the area if they could, rather than have to hear what issued from the home at number I, Vico Storto. They quickly learned not to ask Padre Pio about his "struggles." He wouldn't talk about them. With time, even the doubters had to admit that something "unnatural" was taking place.

Chapter 19

Every community has its misfortunes and its mysteries. In some cases they might even be called horrors. In the quiet town of Pietrelcina, widespread poverty had always been the only misfortune anyone could recall. The only mysteries were those unexplainable events surrounding Padre Pio.

Peasant and country folk are not strangers to superstition. The folklore of the area had its share of goblins, spirits, and spooks. Any villager past the age of four or five knew the old stories well. They'd been handed down through the centuries until no one knew anything about their beginnings. No one took the old tales very seriously. They were just good stories about times past.

When a boy who lived on a farm outside the village reported that he had seen a demon similar to one depicted in local folklore, no one took it too seriously. A few days later another report came from an almost hysterical peasant. A few people began to talk about it. It wasn't until one of the townspeople was found dead just outside Pietrelcina that these events were really taken to heart.

"But there is no proof that **Old Castellino's** death had anything to do with the reports of demons," doubters argued. "There wasn't a mark on him. Granted, he wasn't terribly old, but old enough, what, 62? That's certainly old enough to drop dead."

"Yes, but did you hear about the expression of fright which was on his face when they found him? He must have seen the devil himself."

Among the doubters, there was no stauncher champion than a young peasant named **Agusto Carlino**. He lived and worked in the fields outside Pietrelcina, but after sunset he could be found in town in his favorite tavern, singing, drinking, and commenting on all of the latest gossip of the area. Demonology, of course, was the topic of the month.

The evening's argument was coming to a close when Agusto proclaimed, for everyone present to hear, "If there's a demon out there, let him show himself to me. Tonight I walk the path on which Old Castellino met his death. If that demon wants a chance at me, I'll give it to him. Or perhaps, he'd like to get me as I pass the cemetery along the way. In fact, I think I'll just take the shortcut, through the old graveyard!"

A silence fell. Every eye in the tavern was on Agusto, just where he'd wanted them when he started his boastful and boisterous display. But now that he had issued the challenge, he found in himself a little misgiving. *Well, too bad, I've made the boast and there's no way out.* He waited a moment to see whether the other patrons would talk him out of it, but only silence greeted him. It seemed they were all waiting for him to get up and start his walk. At last one of his friends got up and gave a "Hurrah! That's telling them, Agusto! You'll show 'em. I'll buy you a drink before you go, then you'll show 'em."

Agusto sipped at his drink. When he got to the bottom of the glass it seemed too soon. He was surprised at how anxious he was about the whole situation. When he started his challenge he'd been sincere. He'd had no fear of demons, because he simply didn't believe in them. But from the moment he laid down the challenge, a strange feeling came over him, as if it were there in the room with him, listening, waiting, and savoring. The longer he waited, the stronger the feeling grew. No…it was like a premonition, a premonition of doom.

There was no use putting it off; the longer he waited the harder it would be. Besides, his companions would suspect he was afraid. He gave a look around the room. Every eye was on him. He took a deep breath and stood up, dramatically. "Well, I'm off," and he asked jokingly, "Does anyone care to join me for a walk?" Laughter rang throughout the room. "We'll walk you to the door," someone jested.

Agusto's friend said, "I'll go with you to the edge of town." A few others agreed to do that. It would give them a chance to watch from a safe distance, to make sure he headed into the old graveyard. Once inside, he'd be hidden by the trees and tall tombstones.

Agusto's friend and four others accompanied him to the edge of Pietrelcina, but the whole time Agusto felt there was another, someone, something, felt but unseen. The old graveyard was about a hundred meters from the edge of the village and down a gentle incline. The moon was full and they'd be able to watch him all the way. "What if the gate is closed and locked?" Agusto's friend asked. Agusto had already thought of that. That would give him a feeble excuse to go around instead of through the cemetery. "It is locked," one of the others said, "he'll have to climb over the gate, but that's no problem."

"How will we know you'll go all the way through once you're out of sight?" another asked.

"Where else is there to go, stupid?" Agusto replied, "I tell you what, you come with me. Then you can come back and tell the others." They laughed.

"Why don't you sing for us as you go along the way?" his friend suggested.

Agusto seized the suggestion, "Good idea." It would keep them there. They would be able to hear him singing until he was well past the spot where Old Castellino was found. He took a little comfort in knowing he would have some contact with someone from this world. "I'll sing for you all the way." And again he added in a jesting tone, "And if you should hear a commotion, or if my singing stops, you, all of you come in after me."

As he started down the slope alone he could feel the distance between himself and his friends grow. But the other feeling grew also. The sense that another someone, something was with him. As he sang he strained his ears to listen for footsteps, footsteps he was sure he wouldn't hear. In the distance he could hear his companions' voices fading. The breeze was coming from the cemetery. *That is good*, he thought, *it will carry my sounds to them. Better that they can hear me than I them.* The gate to the old graveyard was now looming up before him. *It is locked. I'll have to climb over to get in. No problem. I'll also have to climb to get out on the other side. As I recall, the wall and gate on that side are higher. It will be more difficult getting out than in.* That was an unhappy thought.

As he climbed the gate he paused in his singing. At the top he looked back. He could see his friends as they stood in the moonlight. He took the opportunity to survey the landscape all around. He saw nothing, no one. He gave a brave wave to his audience and resumed singing, louder now, as he climbed down the Iron Gate on the inside.

It became suddenly obvious that the trees and tombstones that hid him from his friends' view also held out the moonlight. He was plunged into immediate darkness as his feet hit the ground on the inside. It shocked him. For a moment he stopped singing. His throat tightened. His mouth dried. His heart was pounding as if he had a fever. Coldness perched on the back of his neck. The presence was stronger than ever. There was no sound except the wind. It whistled and howled through the trees, like so many ghosts whispering, visiting at their graves. He realized that he was not singing. What would his friends think? *Footsteps? Listen quickly, before you start singing. Look around. Get your bearings. Keep calm; for God's sake keep calm.* He heard no footsteps, saw only shadows; his first attempt to resume his song failed. He swallowed hard, forced up some saliva to wet his mouth, and tried again. The voice was weak, but the breeze carried it to those who listened.

He wanted to run but the darkness prevented it. He might crash into a tree, tombstone, or worse yet, fall into a freshly opened, waiting grave. *Keep calm. There are no demons; they're only in our minds. Just walk, carefully, briskly. It should only take a minute or two to get through this place. Sing louder, they must hear me.* The hair on the back of his neck was like that of a frightened cat.

Clamminess gripped his whole body. And then there was a noise. The song stopped in mid note. *There it is again. Footsteps. It is running. Oh God! What is it? There's no doubt about it, I hear it.* Then the thought came to him, it's those bastards come down to scare me. Sure, that's it. I'll show them. He stopped and crouched down behind a large grave marker.

He heard the running clearly now for a moment over his own breathing, but there was something strange about it. It stopped before he could make it out or pinpoint its location. Now there was silence. What if it's not them?

Up on the hill his friends wondered why the singing had stopped. "I expected as much," one of them said. "He will try to make us think he's in trouble, try to get us down there, then scare the hell out of us. You wait and see if he doesn't start to scream and yell in a minute or two. Then tomorrow he'll joke about the demon that chased him all the way home. Wait, you'll see!"

There was no sound in the graveyard. Agusto's courage began to return. A little moonlight filtered reassuringly through the trees. *You've got to keep calm. Don't let it get to you. Your imagination is your worst enemy.* There was no sound. No footsteps. *Now just get up and slowly walk the rest of the way, singing, calmly. I must be over halfway through. It should take less than a minute now. Just keep calm.*

He stood up and looked around. Terror struck him like a bolt of lightning. There it stood, not twenty meters away. He wanted to scream but couldn't. Before his heart had pounded. Now it felt as if it had stopped. *What is it? It's huge! God, let it be a shadow. I t hasn't moved. Oh God, it must be a shadow or a huge grave marker!*

Slowly he started to back toward the direction he wanted to run. *It must be a shadow. Oh dear God, does it move?* He turned and ran uncontrollably toward the back gate of the graveyard. He could hear it start after him. It began a hideous laugh. He ran faster, not knowing how he kept from crashing into the trees and headstones. "Please, dear God, help me!" He pleaded. The laughter was louder, closer. The gate was just in front of him now. He looked to his side and it was there, running with him stride for stride, laughing, waiting to take him at will. Now a scream broke from Agusto. The creature laughed louder. Agusto reached the gate and jumped up on it, hardly breaking stride as he began to climb. It laughed. As Agusto reached the top of the gate it grabbed him by the ankle. He felt his bowels move, explosively. His mouth dried as if all the fluid drained from his body in that one instant. He had an urge to vomit. Then it let go and started to rattle the gate under him, laughing, louder, harder, roaring laughter, now just roaring.

Agusto fell to the ground on the other side of the gate, motionless.

At first, when Agusto's friends heard the laughter come up from the cemetery, they thought it funny. "Listen to that crazy Agusto. He's teasing us. I've got to admit, I wouldn't have had the nerve. Nothing scares that guy." Even when the scream came on the wind they thought it humorous, the act he was putting on for them, but when the laughter turned to roaring, panic struck at them too. They stood rooted to the ground. None would go down that night to help; to see.

When Agusto was found the next morning he was lying in the exact spot where he fell. The expression on his face was the same mask of terror, a death mask of a horrible end. Not another mark was on the body.

Chapter 20

After Agusto's death there were frequent sightings of demons and monsters. Villagers, farmers, everyone was terrified. The disbelievers no longer taunted the believers. They did not frequent the taverns after dark. No one went outside. When people thought they saw creatures outside through their windows they started closing their shutters. But that didn't keep out the night sounds. Any sound seemed supernatural. Then came reports of the demon rattling at the closed doors and windows outside the shuttered hovels.

After that the talk began. "It is because of Padre Pio. The devil wants him away from here! We will have no peace until he leaves."

It was as if the whole town was possessed. Perhaps it was. Padre Pio understood the people's concern. He went often to the Morgia and prayed. Then he began a ritual of exorcism. He said special blessings and prayers over the people who came to the church. The word spread that Padre Pio's prayers freed those blessed from their fear, danger, and captivity. More people came. The sightings stopped. The nights again became quiet, except around number 1 Vico Storto. There the battles with the devil became almost nightly events. The village took it for granted, took relief in it, for they knew that as long as the demon fought with Padre Pio, they would be safe.

Chapter 21

It was only supposed to be a joke. Stilted boots, an old mask he'd worn a few years earlier to a party. But he had actually scared Agusto to death! **Vito** wished that he'd never left the tavern that night. But he was tired of listening night after night to the loudmouth Agusto. He just wanted to teach him a little lesson. He never imagined the incident would end the way it did. And now the villagers were pointing the blame in poor Padre Pio's direction. But they would never learn the truth.

Chapter 22

Throughout this time no one was more tormented than Gena. She knew it was only a matter of time before she would have to serve the devil again. Adding to her torment were her ambivalent feelings. She could not help looking forward to her dreams for the intense pleasure they gave her, but she felt unfaithful to the husband and family she deeply loved. She felt guilt over the deep lust she felt toward the friar-priest. She dreaded the task before her, yet didn't want to fail again at seducing the man. After Padre Pio freed the town of their fears, Gena's dreams became more frequent, longer, more vivid, and intense. Her time was at hand.

Chapter 23

Padre Pio started sending letters to all of his superiors requesting residency at the friary at San Giovanni Rotondo. He never discussed his reasons for wanting to go. Was it because the people had turned their backs on him during their horror? Perhaps it was because he feared for Pietrelcina and its people. Certainly his encounters must have been a terrible strain on his parents and their neighbors. Whatever the reasons for his request, it was not quickly granted. Pietrelcina was to keep its Padre Pio for some years.

After a time, Padre Pio learned how to hold off his encounters with the devil and shorten the battles when they did occur. It only frustrated the master of demons, and he tried in every way to trick and torment the friar.

In spite of all the problems, or maybe because of them, more and more people flocked to the church of Saint Mary of the Angels to hear Padre Pio's Mass. When he would take their confessions they felt especially blessed. He had a charisma that turned people to the church in droves. Many who never had time for the church before now made time in their busy schedules. As stories spread out from Pietrelcina about the unusual events and the remarkable Capuchin, many jeered and laughed about the far-fetched tales, but in the small town and the surrounding countryside there were few doubters left.

Chapter 24

The day started out almost perfectly. There was a cooling breeze that blew into Pietrelcina, bringing with it a fragrance of wildflowers. There had been a light rain just before dawn to freshen everything. Birds chirped excitedly, as if heralding some great event. The few clouds in the sky glistened white against their bright-blue background. Padre Pio somehow overslept this morning.

Usually he was already out and headed for Saint Mary of the Angels before the first rays of the sun broke over the horizon. It was invigorating to step out into such a lovely morning. He took a deep breath of the aromatic air. A smile crossed his face. He gave a little rub to his bearded chin and started on his way. What could go wrong on a day like this?

Gena also slept later than usual. She'd had another dream during the night but couldn't remember its details. The shutters to her room's window were ajar. Her husband had opened them before he left for his day of toil. The freshness of the morning poured in. Gena stretched, filled her lungs with a deep breath, and jumped from the bed. *It is good to be alive on a day like this.* She poured some water from a pitcher into her basin and washed. She put on her newest sundress, one she would normally keep for special days, for visiting, for a holy day. She had no idea why she chose that dress. It just seemed to be the right dress for this wonderful day.

Padre Pio had only a short time before Mass to devote to his own prayer and meditation because of his tardiness this morning. In the short time he had, his prayers went well. His meditation was deep and undisturbed. Those few minutes alone, with his faith, with his God, left Padre Pio confident that he could face any adversary to goodness. But on a day such as this, a day, which appeared blemish-free, what need would there be for such inner strength?

Gena could hardly wait to get to the church. She wanted to give thanks to God that she was alive this day. She felt a freedom, she knew not from what, but it was an unmistakable burden-free feeling. The fact that she couldn't recall the details of her dream left her conscience untroubled this morning. In fact, gone from her memory were all of the dreams she'd had over the years. Somehow, during the night, all memory of her encounters with the creature, her nocturnal pleasures, her lusting for the friar-priest, and her experience in the Morgia with Francesco, were eradicated from memory. For Gena this day was, indeed, starting out gloriously.

During the service this morning Gena deeply felt her prayers. Never before had she felt such closeness to her God. As Padre Pio led the service he, too, felt something special. *There are days that God sets aside as special days,* he thought in the midst of a silent devotion. *This I feel must be one of those days. What wonder will there occur?* And in that instant he felt an excruciating pain in the palms of both hands, and a heat struck at the tops of both his feet. He wanted to cry out but was able to control himself. He was kneeling before the cross at the time, and as he looked up at the crucified Jesus, a tear ran down his left cheek. Oh my dear Lord, what pain you must have suffered. The tear fell from his cheek to the robe at the lower left chest, and as it did so, he felt a sharp piercing pain under his heart.

It was instantaneous and passed; but it took his breath away and caused him to moan and pitch forward for a second. Of all those congregated, only Gena noticed.

When Padre Pio arose after the silent devotion he felt no pain. He felt good. But as he walked back to his altar he noticed a redness in the palms of both hands, like little burns. He didn't understand, and it troubled him.

Gena sensed his concern and was troubled too.

Several times during the remainder of the service Padre Pio's and Gena's eyes were drawn to each other's. She felt his charisma as a priest as never before. He became aware of the passion of her prayer this day. She felt a love for him as her priest; he felt a love for her as one of his flock. As the service concluded, Padre Pio became aware of an aroma, subtle and unusual, yet strangely familiar. It is floral, but of no flower I recognize, similar to lilacs or roses, but like neither. Where have I experienced that bouquet? He puzzled the question for several moments and then recalled his first vision. That same fragrance accompanied the presence of the Heavenly Father.

A joy came over Padre Pio. The day was indeed marked for something special. He could hardly wait to finish his work here so he could go to his Morgia.

As Gena left the church she turned toward her home. *On such a wonderful day I must be with my family. I will gather together the children, make up a basket of food, some wine, and go with them to the fields and have our noon meal with my dear husband. He works so hard, it will brighten his day.* The thought pleased her. She smiled, started to hum. She strode along like a child at play. And in the next instant she made a sudden turn in the opposite direction. Not knowing why, some power outside herself, or maybe within her, turned her toward the Morgia.

Her radiance of a moment earlier had vanished. Her smile gone, her face was expressionless, staring, blank. Her light, bouncing strides turned into a somnambulistic gait.

As she walked, her will gone, she had a vision. She saw the interior of the Morgia, empty, and herself entering through the opening. There was the familiar cadence of the drumbeat. She went to the dark corner and hid herself in the shadow. Now her passions began to grow. She felt a blush pass through her body, leaving a glow in her breasts and the pit of her stomach, passing from there down and into her womb. She felt an urgency in her pubis. She tore at her clothing until she was free of it. Naked, she fell to the straw where she'd seen Francesco kneel years before.

She writhed in the floor covering hay, driven by a passion she'd never felt before. She felt an emptiness she needed filled. Her desire panicked her. She pressed herself with her hand to relieve the need, but it only heightened. Momentarily, she rubbed and her passion exploded, but it gave her only a few seconds of relief and again started to build, to tantalize, to torment…

And then a gruff voice whispered into her ear, "You will know no peace until you have the priest. You will not fail. He will be seduced by your passion for him. You will have him. You will have him this day. You will serve me when you serve him. He comes to you soon."

The hypnotic tone of the words only increased the pitch of her lust. Again she pressed, rubbed, massaged, and found only temporary relief. Again and again she sought to satisfy herself, but each time her torment became greater. Only Padre Pio would free her of this lust.

On his way to the Morgia Padre Pio also had a foreshadowing, a premonition. As he approached, another aroma presented itself, an odor not unlike excrement, but not human or animal in nature. It grew stronger as he neared the shack. A voice broke the silence, "Beware, the stench of the devil. He awaits you." And then the odor faded and was replaced by the bouquet he noticed in the church, and the voice returned, "Fear not, for you are not alone."

Before entering his Morgia Padre Pio stopped and evoked a blessing on the building and all that was inside. Upon its completion a hideous wail emerged, and then only the pitiful sounds of a woman crying, a weak sobbing, like that of a small, lost child.

Padre Pio entered the Morgia. The stench was gone. He saw Gena crying on the floor. She was ashamed of her nakedness before him. He covered her with her dress. Kneeling, he performed a ritual of exorcism over her, freeing her forever of her affliction and taking upon himself one more curse of the devil.

Chapter 25

In May of 1915, Italy entered World War I, allied with England, France, and Russia against Germany and Austria. Padre Pio was twenty-eight and still living in Pietrelcina, awaiting appointment to permanent residency to San Giovanni Rotondo. His neighbors and parishioners at the church of Saint Mary of the Angels were used to his frequent nightly struggles with demons and the devil. It didn't frighten them anymore. They felt it kept them safe. They adored his Mass, now that he controlled the length so that they could get to the fields in time to do all their work. Sundays the little church overflowed. Confession to Padre Pio was something special. The people wanted him to stay. The slowness of his superiors to act pleased them. But now, in 1915, war interceded.

His mother, Giuseppe, received the letter addressed to Francesco Forgione. In 1915 Italy there was no such thing as exemption from the service. All able-bodied males were eligible, and though Padre Pio was still plagued by frequent bouts of respiratory disease and unbelievably high fevers, he was called up for his induction physical exam "by order of **King Victor Emanuel II."**

"Mama, it is nothing to worry over. It states that I am to report to Naples for examination. It is my duty. God will be with me. If it is His will that I serve I will serve. If not, I will not have to." It was God's will. Padre Pio, in spite of his physical afflictions, passed his medical exam without reservation. Everyone who knew the priest was flabbergasted that he was found acceptable for military service. None thought he would ever wear the uniform. Only Padre Pio was not surprised. All along he assured them he would pass the physical. To him it was still another trial to endure; the will of God, preordained, an area where his services were needed, his holy obligation. "It has nothing to do with war, or nation, or King Victor; it matters only that there is suffering out there, and I can help my fellow man… "

Padre Pio was assigned to the Tenth Company of the Medical Corps in the fall of 1915. He was stationed at the hospital **Trinita dei Monti**, in Naples, as an orderly. His habit and sandals were locked away, and he was given the standard gray-green uniform of an Italian soldier. For at least his part of the war, he was now **Private Francesco Forgione.**

He was barracked with thirty other soldiers. His bed was a cot. The complaints of poor food, hard beds, long hours, and low military pay were no ordeal for Padre Pio. His burden was the suffering of the wounded, the death he witnessed daily, the inhumanity and lack of compassion around him everywhere. For him the days were too short for all he wanted to accomplish. It was difficult to find time for his prayer and meditation. He began to feel unworthy because of his frustration. He went to his cot late in the night, exhausted, and arose hours before the duty call to go to the **Shrine of Caesarea** on **the Via Salvatore Rosa** to celebrate Mass at the altar of **Our Lady of Patience.**

Regardless of how heavy a workload Padre Pio took upon himself, there was always more to do. He started to skip meals to give himself more time for the suffering men. He disregarded his own health. The other personnel could not believe the effort this man put forth. He worked two or more shifts a day, ate nothing, took no breaks from his toil, slept only one or two hours a night, seemed tireless, and had a compassion such as none they had ever known. When his superiors demanded, ordered that he rest, his reply was, "God prepares my duty roster; He will determine when I need my rest."

One night a request came for a truck to pick up a wounded officer from a smaller hospital and transfer him to Trinita dei Monti. A driver and an orderly were needed. The doctor in charge assigned Private Francesco Forgione to go. He did it to give the orderly a break. Since he wouldn't leave the wards when ordered to rest, maybe he'd get some rest on the three hour ride to the other hospital. Anyway, the change of scenery would be good for him. It was dusk when the truck left on its trip up the west coast of Italy. They rumbled along for about an hour. The road was narrow, rough, and winding. It snaked in and out along its route. Just about the time they were heading into the most remote area along the way the driver started to get nervous. Padre Pio sensed his anxiety immediately. "What is it? Something bothers you, my friend."

"I feel a strange vibration in the motor. I doesn't run smoothly."

"I am afraid I know nothing of motors," Padre Pio mentioned,

"I will be of no help to you." They drove on only a little further when a loud rattling noise started up from under the hood. At the same time Padre Pio became aware of a putrid smell. "What is that?"

"The noise? I am afraid to guess," the driver replied.

"No, not the rattle, that odor."

The driver sniffed at the air, "I smell nothing!"

Padre Pio was certain of its presence, and now he recognized where he'd experienced it before. It had been outside the Morgia the day he performed the exorcism over Gena. Now he knew. The devil was riding with them.

"What is the importance of this mission we are on?" he asked the driver.

"We are to pick up a high-ranking officer, gravely injured. He is at a remote hospital where they can give him little help. Also they have no priest there, and though he probably cannot be saved, he does not want to die without making his peace with the Lord. Too bad they aren't so considerate with the fighting men."

Padre Pio ignored the sarcasm of the last remark, "We must get through to him; he is a soul in pain."

At the moment he said that, the odor became stronger to Padre Pio, the rattle became louder, and there was a sudden and loud report from under the hood. The truck lurched and started to coast to a stop. "Damn!" the driver exclaimed. "I think we've blown our engine. What a God-forsaken place this is. Now we're really stuck."

"Stuck we may be," Padre Pio replied, "but 'God-forsaken' does not exist in the universe."

"Well I think you'll change your mind about that," the driver commented as he jumped from the open cab to look under the motor. Padre began to pray.

"Damn!" came up from under the truck, "we've blown a rod right through the bottom of the oil pan. We'll be here for the rest of the war!"

Padre Pio continued his prayer. A few minutes later a motorcyclist came along. "I'll take a message to the next town and send you back help," he offered.

"How long will it take for them to come back for us?" the driver asked.

"I doubt you'll see anyone before dawn," the cyclist replied. "I'd like to help you more, but I know nothing of trucks, and I go no further than the next village."

"You can do no more for us. Getting help will do. We must stay with our truck. It is regulations," the driver announced.

Padre Pio was very disturbed about the delay. A distressed soul waited. The friar kneeled at the side of the road to pray.

"Crazy," the driver mumbled to himself, "does he think God will come and fix the motor?" He went to a grassy spot at the base of a tree and sat down, making himself as comfortable as possible. He looked over at the kneeling private in his oversized uniform. *Ridiculous sight; look at the nut. Huh! Oh well, let him do as he pleases. Won't hurt me any.* He leaned back against the tree and looked up at the moon. It was in its first quarter. *Nice enough night. If we have to be stuck, at least it's comfortable.* He looked back at the friar. He hadn't moved a fraction. *Kind of eerie*, the driver thought. *Like a damned statue. Never seen anything like that. Never seen anyone who could hold that still.* He watched for several minutes, looking for the slightest motion. *Uncanny. I don't believe what I'm seeing. He's been motionless for fifteen minutes. Not a move, not a sound. Just like a damned statue*. "Hey, are you all right?" he called out, but he got no answer. *Damned weird.* He sat for ward and squinted a little, then shrugged and sat back again.

"Well, it ain't hurtin' me none," he mumbled.

Ten minutes later Padre Pio moved for the first time. The driver saw him cross himself and then rise off of his knees. He looked about and finally, locating the driver in the darkness, walked over to the tree.

"Well, did you solve our problem with your prayer?"

"It will be fine now."

"What'll be fine?"

"Everything…we'll be picked up soon by another truck that will tow us clear to the other hospital. We'll leave our truck in that town for repairs and an ambulance will arrive from farther north and take us and our patient back to Trinita dei Monti." The driver looked at the orderly in amazement. He didn't know whether he was being kidded or just taken for a fool. He didn't know just how to reply. Finally he said, "And just what makes you so sure our patient will still be alive in the morning?"

"He will be all right."

The driver just looked at his travel companion, shook his head, leaned back against the tree, and closed his eyes. *Crazy fool.*

Not an hour had passed before a truck came along the road. Its horn awoke the sleeping driver. "What's your trouble?" the other driver called down from his cab. It was another military vehicle.

"Engine threw a rod," the first driver answered, getting up from where he'd been snoozing. "Can you help?"

"Where you goin'?"

"Hospital about fifty miles north of here."

Padre Pio just sat and listened to the conversation between the two military drivers as if they were reading from a script he'd been privy to.

"That's where I'm headed. I've got chains. We'll hook up and I'll tow you there. That's where our motor pool is stationed.

They'll repair you there."

Padre Pio's driver turned slowly to his passenger and stared in bewilderment. "Ye ... Yes, that will be fine… "

They arrived at the smaller hospital, a primitive place, just at dawn. The night staff was still there-a doctor, two nurses, and an orderly. As Pio and the driver entered, the doctor and one of the nurses greeted in unplanned unison, ' 'Good morning, Padre."

"Good morning, how is the patient?"

"Much improved since you were here last night, Padre. Almost like a miracle. But why aren't you in your robe and sandals today?"

"Today I am here as an orderly."

The driver couldn't say a word. He thought himself half mad. What was this talk about?

"May I see the patient?" Padre Pio asked.

"Of course," the other nurse answered, "he has already asked for you several times. He is convinced you saved his life during the night."

The doctor interjected, "I'm of the same opinion, Padre. It would have been miracle enough for him to have survived the night, but he is remarkably better, as if cured by your prayer." Padre Pio started down the hall; the driver followed, mouth open.

Chapter 26

After several months at his inhuman pace, Padre Pio began his fevers again. His lungs ached when he breathed. He coughed, and his sputum became blood-tinged. The nurses noticed his condition first, and when one took his temperature at the end of a day she made him lie down and called for the nearest doctor. "What did you say his fever was?" the physician asked.

"I don't know sir, it went off the scale of our thermometer."

"Well, that's impossible. Let's try another one." The doctor placed it under the priest's tongue, inadvertently touching his cheek.

"Oh!" He touched the man's forehead, carefully. "I can't believe how hot you feel. It actually hurts to touch you. In just a few seconds the thermometer read off the scale. "Nurse, get me a laboratory thermometer. In less than a minute of placing it under Padre Pio's arm, it registered 125 degrees.

Over the next few days every physician in the hospital examined Padre Pio. This time he was not delirious. He actually wanted to get up and do his work, but his superiors would hear nothing of it. Some of the doctors insisted the friar had an atypical case of tuberculosis; others insisted it could not be TB. All agreed that the temperatures were incompatible with life. But indeed the man lived. All agreed that he would be dead within the week, if not days or hours. After a week more they decided to give him a "furlough" home, they were sure, to die. They would send for him in a few months, if he were still alive, and decide then how to reassign him.

Padre Pio returned to Pietrelcina, his parents' home, Saint Mary of the Angels, and his Morgia.

While he waited for his reassignment, the Provincial Father sent him to San Giovanni Rotondo. Pio would petition for permanent residence there and also spend some time meditating.

Days passed into weeks and then months. No notice came from the military. At last, after six months, a letter came to Padre's mother in Pietrelcina, addressed to Private Francesco Forgione. She forwarded it to San Giovanni Rotondo. There the postmaster returned it to its sender stating that no Francesco Forgione lived in the province. This brought out the King's police with a warrant for Private Francesco Forgione's arrest as a deserter. They first went to his home in Pietrelcina. From there they were directed to San Giovanni Rotondo. At that point the Captain of Province Police was employed to search for the deserter. He knew of no one by that name, but agreed to help. For days they searched and questioned.

Not until one of the friars, in town to deliver some food to an ailing woman, hearing the name inadvertently mentioned, cleared up the mystery.

Padre Pio did not pass his reassignment physical and was returned to San Giovanni Rotondo.

Chapter 27

Don Salvatore Pannullo, the archpriest of Pietrelcina, was nearing the end of his story to Brother Gaudenzio. "After he finished his military obligation, officially, he returned to your friary, as you know. Of course you know the rest better than I. His request for permanent residency there was granted on June 5, 1918. We have missed him here. Now it is you who must tell me what has happened."

Part II.

Chapter 28

Brother Gaudenzio spoke to Don Salvatore of the events that had taken place on September 20, 1918. He told it as it had been told to him, "I shall try to tell you, as near as I can remember, in Padre's own words. He told us, 'I was kneeling in the **Coro** before the small wooden crucifix I so much love. You know, the small one which is but three feet high and so thick.'

At that point he held up his hand and showed a space of about an inch between his thumb and forefinger. "My eyes were, of course immediately drawn to the bandage on his hand, which was already soaked through with his blood." He put his hand down and went on with his tale. "'Its painted image of Jesus seemed so real this morning, showing every muscle and rib in detail, as if alive. I'd never realized the depth of agony in its contorted face. It was as if I were seeing this, my favorite crucifix, for the first time. Tears welled in my eyes as I looked upon the spikes driven through the hands and feet.

"'Then without warning a feeling swept over me. A peace like none I'd ever known. It was almost like a sweet sleep. All external senses ceased. I was engulfed in an external numbness, yet a new sensation penetrated my every fiber internally. I felt a complete abandonment of everything worldly. There was total silence. It was as if I had been miraculously suspended in a vacuum, only the crucifix looming before me. Nothing else existed.

'"All at once my eyes opened wide in terror. The crucifix was coming to life before me. Bright light blinded me to everything but the figure growing to enormous dimensions. The being before me was dripping blood. It collected in pools where I knelt. My heart pounded as never before, surely on the verge of bursting. Then it appeared as if arrows and lances were bursting toward me from somewhere behind the figure, and all began to fade. I felt myself falling, splashing into the pool of blood at my knees.

'"I am unaware of the time I lay there. Sensation was returning. I felt a quivering in my limbs, then a dull ache which quickly turned to a sharp pain, stabbing repeatedly at my hands, my feet, at my chest. My back burned as if I'd been whipped. I looked to my hand and saw it bleeding. I raised to one elbow and saw that I was soaked in blood. Horror gripped me. Trying to rise, I slipped back into the blood, which now seemed to surround me. I was driven to get out of the Coro, to the sanctuary of my cell, to the security of my little bed…

'"Each step was an agony. Some strength other than mine helped me. I collapsed to my sheets, trying to understand. I wanted to scream ... Father, please take away my fear, my pain. Let me understand ... and before another second passed I felt peace. My fear vanished. The pain remained, but was bearable.

'"I looked down at all my wounds and understood that I bore the stigmata… '

"Not until then," Brother Gaudenzio continued, "did he realize the presence of **Brother Agostino** in his cell with him. He was still unaware that we had been witness to part of his ordeal. Had helped him to his cell."

Chapter 29

When Brother Gaudenzio returned to San Giovanni Rotondo, he found the friary cloaked in secrecy. Brother Nicola had of course returned from his short trip to Foggia and the Provincial Father, but no instructions had yet come back from that authority.

"How do you hope to keep such a thing as the stigmata a secret?" Brother Gaudenzio asked. "Why would you want such a blessing kept from the people?"

"Yes, it is a blessing," the Guardian Father, Brother Agostino replied. "Perhaps it is the greatest religious event of the century, but we must treat it carefully. If we are premature its repercussions could be far-reaching and perhaps harmful. There will be doubters. There will be those who want to exploit. There is much that we cannot foresee. We must have time to think of these things and to prepare. This news must reach the proper authorities by proper channels. It would not do for rumor to herald such a holy happening."

Back at Pietrelcina, Don Salvatore took no such precautions. He spoke openly and with pride of the events surrounding his young protégé. He would think later, Perhaps I was committing the sin of boastfulness; Perhaps I was taunting the devil!

The response he got from his parishioners bordered ridicule: "You don't really believe what you speak, do you?"

"Things like that do not happen in our times."

"You have been deceived by trickery. These are modern times. True, there have been many mysteries surrounding Padre Pio, but the stigmata, that goes too far."

Some believed. Most didn't. Don Salvatore took the doubt as a personal affront. "You who don't believe, you forget so quickly."

"But things like this do not really occur."

The archpriest's face reddened. He pointed his finger accusingly and cried out, "Then you don't believe **Saint Francis of Assisi was stigmatized**?"

"Of course he was, but that is different!"

"How?"

"That was long ago, in times when such strange things still happened." Then the doubter spoke on, "Padre, if you were to go to San Giovanni and see this for yourself and return still believing, then I would believe."

Don Salvatore decided to do just that. A day later he left for the monastery, and with him about half of the people of Pietrelcina. It was the first of many pilgrimages to Saint Mary of the Graces.

When the pilgrims reached San Giovanni, the people of that town still had no idea what had happened. But the word spread rapidly. Now there was no stopping it. Travelers carried it to Foggia, only a few miles away.

Despite the shield of silence the friars, Padre Pio, and his superiors tried to maintain, the stories gained momentum. Soon all of Italy knew. And what the Guardian Father feared came true.

The press picked up the story and sensationalized it. It spread to the rest of the world. Because of the sensationalism and distortion of facts, many priests attacked Padre Pio in their sermons, letters, and articles. Those who knew better, and they were few in number, defended the Capuchin. In any case, he became legend overnight.

Chapter 30

As rumors spread and legends were born, the **Father Provincial** mounted a full investigation of the matter. The Church would make no statement, either in support or denial of Padre Pio, without complete examination.

On September 28, 1918, a visitor presented himself at the gate of the monastery, which had remained locked since the event. He was burdened by huge cases of equipment. Perspiration stood heavy on his brow and soaked his clothing after carrying the load up the narrow, treacherous, and winding mountain road from San Giovanni Rotondo to the cloister. His first knock on the thick, wooden door was feeble. He rested, waiting for an answer that did not come. In the time he waited he regained a little of his strength. The sun reflected off of the high, whitewashed, adobe wall that surrounded the centuries-old edifice, and he sweltered. Thirst choked him. The hot air he breathed parched his throat. Impatience overcame his fatigue and he knocked vigorously at the locked door. Not even an echo. Frustrated, he looked up and down the great wall for another entrance. Not until then did he notice a rope pull at the edge of the door, just behind him.

Exasperated at his own foolishness, he gave it a vigorous tug. A bell on the inside sounded, echoing between the building and its surrounding barricade. *No doubt they'll hear that*, he thought. *That should raise the dead.* At least another minute passed before he heard quick footsteps approaching the door from the inside. "Who is there, please? This area is not for public entrance at the present."

"I am sent by the Father Provincial, Padre. I am here to photograph Padre Pio. It is official, my visit."

There was a short silence while the friar contemplated what he had heard, and then a heavy bolt could be heard moving through the door. At its removal, the door swung open only an inch or two, and an eye peered out. It looked first at the man, then scanned the bulky equipment piled about his feet. Another second of decision-making passed, and then the door swung open the rest of the way.

"I am sorry, but we must take precaution. Were we not careful we'd be overrun by the curious. I assume you have a letter of introduction from the Father Provincial."

The photographer said nothing but reached into his inner coat pocket and withdrew a sealed envelope. It was soggy with perspiration, and the man was a bit embarrassed to hand it over. "I am sorry about its condition, but the trip up here was hot and difficult."

"Never mind that, my son," the friar replied, taking the envelope. "I see it has the Father's seal, unbroken. That is all that matters." The friar opened the letter and read its contents. He seemed satisfied. "Won't you come with me. Let me help you carry your burden."

The door was closed and bolted behind the visitor. "Where would you like to do your work?" the friar asked.

"Wherever there is good light."

"The garden then."

"That would be fine, if it is alright with Padre Pio."

"Padre Pio will do as the Father Provincial has instructed. He will cooperate with you in any way his conscience will allow."

While the photographer set up his equipment the friar went to get Padre Pio.

The photographer was not a particularly religious man. He was chosen for the job because he was the only person in the immediate area with the talent and equipment. When he found out he would have to carry everything up the mountain himself he was not pleased. He'd heard all the rumors and was not impressed by them. It never occurred to him that he was given the honor of being the first person in the entire world, outside of the Capuchin friars in the cloister, to lay eyes upon the stigmata. He gave no thought to the fact that thousands of people the world over would have given anything to be in his place. Instead, he became hostile on his wearying journey up the hill. In his imagination he played out dozens of scenarios where he would put these religious fanatics in their places. He'd expose this scam, become famous, sell his photos to the press, and perhaps begin a lecture tour.

Once set up in the garden, he had to wait for Padre Pio. His hostility mounted. *They wilI probably insist I keep a distance from the priest. Well I'll insist otherwise. I'll make them let me take close photographs of the wounds. They'll not fool my camera or me. If they want me to be a party to this, then they'll have to pay.*

Padre Pio entered the garden from the far side. He limped and shuffled along, moving in obvious pain. As soon as the photographer saw Padre Pio a feeling of awe came over him. In spite of the pain he could see the man bearing, there was an expression of peace on his face. *Even if those wounds are self-inflicted, they must be terribly painful*, the visitor thought. When Padre Pio's eyes met the photographer's, the friar smiled through his suffering, a smile that warmed the visitor to the friar. Without a word Padre Pio's charisma touched the doubter's heart. He felt instantly humbled by the presence of the friar-priest.

In the privacy of the garden the photographer was allowed to take all the photographs he wanted, from any distance and angle. When he left he could hardly wait to tell his fellow townspeople of the magnificent priest with the stigmata that graced their province.

Chapter 31

The first physician to visit and examine Padre Pio was **Dr. Luigi Romanelli.** He arrived at the monastery on October 9, 1918, at the request of the Provincial Father of the Minor Capuchin Brothers. If ever there was a man skeptical of the authenticity of the stigmata, it was Dr. Luigi Romanelli. A man of science, of considerable renown, he was not about to accept the word of such an affliction on faith alone. The stigmata, if true, would break all physiologic and pathologic rules, would have no precedent or explanation under scientific law, and would not fit under any natural phenomenon. There was no place for such an event in the mind of this physician.

Dr. Romanelli was disarmed at the first examination. He could not bring himself to believe the results of his investigation. He would not believe. "I am not ready to draw my conclusion," he stated at the end of his visit. "I will have to make several more examinations. Today I have seen the lesions and have made notes and measurements. I must see how the wounds progress. I would like to return in a few days and repeat my examination."

Padre Pio agreed to put himself at the physician's disposal.

Four times Dr. Luigi Romanelli, of the **Barletta Civilian Clinic**, examined Padre Pio during the month of October 1918. Finally he delivered his report to the

Provincial Father. It was nine hundred words long, and concluded; "I do not find clinical evidence that would authorize me to classify the five wounds on the person of Padre Pio in any known medical terms or syndromes."

In that same report, Dr. Luigi Romanelli gave the first scientific descriptions of the five lesion's- measurements that would be repeated over the years by many men of science, always with compatible and reproducible results.

He wrote, "Padre Pio has a very deep cut at the fifth intercostal space on the left side, 7 to 8 ems. long and running parallel to the ribs. It is in the shape of an upside down cross. Its depth is too great to ascertain, as it is in the direction of the base of the heart. The wounds of the hands issue an abundance of arterial blood. The borders of the wounds show no inflammation. There is severe pain at the least pressure. The lesions of the hands are covered with a dark red membrane, but there is no edema or infection. When I press my fingers on the palms and backs of his hands there is a sensation of an empty space.

"The lesions of the feet have the same characteristics as those on the hands, but because of the thickness of the foot, it was more difficult to experiment as accurately on the feet as on the hands."

The Church Superiors were not to be satisfied by the report of just THIS one physician. Over the next several years, repeated examinations were carried out. About a year later, on October 9, 1919, they commissioned a physician and surgeon, **Dr. Giorgio Festa**, to examine Padre Pio. He came from Rome and was by reputation one of that city's finest physicians.

After his examination he wrote; "I found Padre Pio to be a jovial patient, cooperative and willing to submit to evaluation in every way, even when it meant the procedure would elicit pain.

"His weight at the time of my examination was 169 lbs, his height 5 feet and 10 inches, though his bulky habit makes him look larger and heavier. When he disrobes one sees that he is slight of build. His skin is pale. I was surprised to see that he had excoriations and abrasions on his back, some of them weeping blood, similar to those seen on one who has been whipped. He reported to me that this was also a part of his stigmata, a fact not commonly known and not previously reported.

"In the palm of his hand, at a point corresponding with the middle of his third metacarpal, I saw the existence of an anatomical lesion, round in shape, with clearly defined outer edges. In size it is a little more than 2 ems. in diameter. The lesions are covered with a reddish brown membrane. The wounds are continuously bloody.

"Examination under high-powered magnification shows no sign of edema, inflammation or infection. There are no signs of having been struck, irritated, teased, chemically treated, or for that matter of any form of continuing trauma.

"When asked to make a fist, he could not close his hands completely. On the feet the lesions are similar. In both cases the lesions on the top of the feet are larger than those on the bottoms.

"The chest lesion looks like an upside-down cross, 7 ems. long, at the fifth rib of the left chest. It slants down toward the cartilage. Again there is no trace of edema, inflammation, infection, or tampering. This wound produces constant droplets of blood before my eyes, and in quantity greater than the other wounds."

But there was something the good Dr. Festa failed to put in his report. On his train ride back to Rome, a strange thing occurred. As he gazed at the countryside, which passed by his window, his thoughts fell on Padre Pio. Pio had told Dr. Festa as he was leaving the monastery that he would pray that he would have a safe journey home. Dr. Festa leaned back in his seat and rested his head on his pillow. It was a warm gesture from Pio, but he wondered how, with all the other people begging for prayers from the holy ma, Pio would find the time. At that moment a delicate fragrance, like that of lilacs except much more beautiful, entered his nostrils. Because Dr. Festa had habitual nosebleeds as a child, his sense of smell was almost nil. It had been a long time since he had sensed such an aroma. For no specific reason, the doctor reached down to the floor for his medical bag. When he opened it, the scent assailed him. It was emitting from a cloth bandage he had removed from the padre. He was taking it home with him so that he could examine the dried blood sample under a microscope.

There was a buzzing in the car. Dr. Festa looked up to see the other passengers looking about, obviously to pinpoint the source of the sweet aroma. He tucked the piece of cloth back in the bag and replaced it on the floor. To avoid calling attention to himself, he began looking around the car also. Then he sat back and chuckled. "Thank you for your prayers, Padre," he mumbled.

The report of this incident would eventually reach the **Holy Office**, but it wouldn't be until Dr. Festa began receiving comments from the patients who visited him at his place of practice about the strange fragrance, which pervaded his office. None of them knew about the old bandage tucked away deeply in his desk drawer.

Chapter 32

Victoro Francelli was a young man of San Giovanni Rotondo. He was hard working, devoutly religious, betrothed to his boyhood sweetheart, and in awe of Padre Pio. He was literate and an avid reader. His family had little money to spend on his education, but he was bright and educated himself with books that he purchased used, borrowed, or begged. Padre Pio had met him when he first came to the monastery. He'd been Victoro's confessor and talked with him often in the gardens. Padre Pio collected books to nurture Victoro's fertile mind, and a fast friendship developed between the two. Victoro chose Padre Pio to be his religious guide and mentor. When Padre Pio first received the stigmata, Victoro cried, initially because of his friend's suffering, then with joy for his priest's glory. When all the controversy arose over the authenticity of the stigmata, Victoro Francelli became Padre Pio's staunchest supporter.

Victoro had apprenticed to the leading cobbler of San Giovanni and thus was known to most of the citizenry, as well as to many of the peasants from the surrounding countryside. When the old cobbler died, most of his customers remained with Victoro, who took over the shop. Not only was he an excellent tradesman, but he agreed to help the old cobbler's widow out of his earnings, an obligation he took on his own, it not being a requirement of his contract with his mentor. When word spread of his act of charity it gained him great loyalty among the cobbler shop's patrons.

Victoro had the respect of almost all who knew him; the envy of those very few who knew him and didn't admire him. Even the rabble of the town liked him for his understanding, compassion, and willingness to accept people for what they were. His character could have made him a civic leader, had he wanted to pursue such ambitions.

Victoro's wedding had been scheduled for November of 1918, just two months after the advent of Padre Pio's stigmata. The couple hoped that Padre Pio's intention of performing their wedding ceremony would not have to change. Padre Pio hoped the same.

Late in October, on a brisk fall day, Victoro left his mother's house, where he still lived, to head for his shop. It was a day like most that week. Nothing had been different up to the time he left home. He'd been cheerful, even remarked what a fine sleep he'd had. He kissed his mother goodbye, as he did daily, and told her he was going to Mass, as usual, at the small chapel between home and his shop.

Still early in the morning, he met few people on the street yet, but that was not unusual either. Those who remembered seeing him that morning mentioned that he'd greeted them with his usual cordiality. He was missed at Mass that morning period. The cobbler shop never opened again.

A short distance before Victoro reached the church there was a slight turn in the road that prevented one from seeing beyond. Just before rounding that turn

Victoro became aware of a putrid odor, such as he'd never experienced before. He had an immediate urge to vomit. He looked quickly around and saw no one. He leaned against a tree and retched, emptying his stomach. He became very dizzy and his head ached as if being crushed. His vision blurred and dimmed. A loud whirring sound pained his ears. Perspiration flowed off him and a severe cutting cramp struck at him in the pit of his stomach. He hardly had the strength to stand. He wanted to scream but could barely gasp in sufficient breath to sustain himself. A fierce wind seemed to be whirling around him he thought, perhaps, around him alone.

Then, as suddenly as it had struck at him, the odor vanished. His pain went with the wind, as did the whirring noise. His vision returned to reveal that no one was around to witness his plight. He had no hint of nausea and all that remained of his profuse sweating was dampness in his clothing. He actually felt wonderful. To him, the day seemed more wonderful than before. He sensed a freedom he'd never felt in the past, as if he hadn't a care in the world.

He continued on the road, around the bend, a lightness to his step. He passed in front of the church, not giving a single thought to the Mass he'd not missed in years. He lavished in a feeling of irresponsibility he'd never known before. Just as he'd passed the church without a thought, so he went by his shop, with not so much as a sideward glance. He continued to the edge of town to a tavern he'd never patronized.

Almost everyone in the tavern recognized the new customer. He sat alone at a corner table drinking an extraordinary quantity of wine. He talked to himself, laughed outrageously, and yelled out profanities with increasing frequency. He seemed intoxicated, but somehow not by the wine. At first those who couldn't believe their eyes left him to himself. Finally one of the town rowdies, emboldened by curiosity, went to Victor's table. When the others saw that he was welcomed, asked to join in and treated to drink, they too went over. Soon that distant corner was the site of a boisterous party. Victoro only insisted that *"ladies of the tavern"* filled the two seats on either side of him.

As the day bore on, one after another of his new companions fell away, too drunk to continue, yet Victoro, who out drank them all, continued. As one left, another took his or her place. As the time passed, word spread through the town of Victoro Francelli's bizarre behavior. Many of the townspeople walked the distance to the tavern just to look in and confirm in their own minds what they could not believe. A few entered and tried to persuade their friend to leave. They were sent away with profanities of untold color.

When the old cobbler's widow heard the unbelievable news she sent a male friend, for a woman of proper breeding would not enter such a place, to get Victoro out of "that place in which he was surely being held against his own will."

The friend, though somewhat past his prime, was still a giant of a man and well chosen to help Victoro out of a place he couldn't possibly want to stay.

He entered the tavern and easily caught sight of Victoro who was singing loudest among his new friends. It seemed that half the town had followed the intervener to the tavern, and they crowded at the door to watch what would happen.

"Victoro," the man called out over the din. "Victoro! Vie-toro!

The last he bellowed like a bull. It caught everyone's attention. "Victoro, the widow sent me here to get you out of this place." Victoro looked up at the man who fully expected him to seize the opportunity to escape these fiends. Silence surrounded the group that had moments before been engulfed in merriment. The cobbler broke the silence with, "Better you give the widow your cock, you old son-of-a-bitch, then give me her unwanted advice!"

The giant's mouth dropped open as he registered what had just been told him. Then his face reddened and he lost control of himself. He was easily twice Victoro's weight and at least half a foot taller. He lunged at the man who had just insulted him and his widow friend. Victoro had never been known as a man of violence, but as the hulking man charged him he jumped up from the table, up-ending it, and caught the man by his collar. With one hand he virtually lifted him off of the floor. In the next move he flung the giant across the room toward the door. The human projectile bowled over the stunned townspeople watching in the doorway as he flew through. Victoro emitted a coarse laugh and sat down at another table.

Chapter 33

Padre Pio was restricted to the friary and not allowed to serve parishioners directly. The news of his friend Victoro reached the monastery by early afternoon. Brother Nicola was appointed to tell Padre Pio of it. Brother Nicola dreaded the task and made his way slowly up the stairs and down the long corridor to cell number five. He knocked and was asked in by Padre Pio. Tears were in Padre Pio's eyes.

"Are you in serious pain Padre?" Nicola asked.

"Not worse than usual, the tears are for my friend Victoro."

"But who told you?"

"That was for you to do," Padre Pio replied, "but you needn't dread it any longer. I have seen it all."

Brother Nicola didn't even bother to ask for an explanation. He'd been too often amazed by such feats. "How can we help your friend? Surely there is some way."

Padre Pio lowered his head sorrowfully, "Not yet. We are each compelled to play our roles until the proper time. We can only pray there not be too much suffering."

Victoro's fiancée was grief-stricken when she heard. She couldn't believe the rumors. Her father believed. He was one of those who saw. He cancelled the wedding immediately. Victoro's mother was nearly in shock. How can this be? She struggled up the mountain to the church of Saint Mary of the Graces to see Padre Pio, but there she found that he was not allowed to see her. Brother Nicola held council with her and promised to take her message to the only priest she believed could help her. The substitute friar was deeply concerned that the elderly lady would not be able to survive this terrible ordeal. "What greater pain can there be than that of seeing one's child go astray?" he asked Padre Pio.

The next morning Victoro's mother was a changed woman.

During the night Padre Pio had visited her. It was at the same time that the priest had knelt before his favorite crucifix in the chapel of the cloister. After her visitation she had all the faith and inner strength she would need to face her ordeal.

That same night, Victoro was taking pleasures from several of the tavern girls. Inhibition was unknown that night. It was his first experience with unbridled lust. At first they showed him pleasures that he never knew existed, then some force took hold of him, and he performed acts that even he had never imagined. There were three girls, and together they could not satisfy his appetite. He satiated each of them in turn then went back out to continue his drinking.

Chapter 34

In the town of San Giovanni Rotondo, a grotesque figure slithered unsteadily down a narrow side street. The villagers shunned it, turning their heads in repulsion.

"Why do his parents let him out of his home?"

"He belongs in a circus side-show."

"How can they allow him to make such a spectacle of himself?"

"I hear there are special places for freaks such as he."

The deformed figure was that of **Clemente Alatando**, age fourteen. He had been born a hunchback. So acute was the curvature of his spine, he was unable to even stand. Instead, he would drag himself around on his knees and elbows. Sometimes he found it easier to roll. It broke his mother's heart seeing him confined within the walls of their tiny home, so she would leave the door open and remain silent as Clemente slowly made his way toward the fresh air and warm, sun-baked ground of the outside world. Maybe God will see him today.

Clemente was approximately eight blocks away from his house when it happened. He thought maybe he'd been struck by lightning, but there was no sound. The blinding light remained for what seemed like several seconds. He felt a hand on his shoulder. Turning his head upward and squinting his eyes to the intense glare, he saw the monk.

The next moment Clemente found himself standing upright. The monk, along with the bright light, had vanished. *I'm on my feet! I'm on my feet!* Tears welled in his eyes. He took a step, then another, and another. Trying to run, he stumbled, but steadied himself before falling. It would take him a while to learn to balance himself properly. Finding it easier to take smaller steps, he started toward home. A passer-by, seeing how wobbly his gait was, asked him if he were drunk. Clemente stopped, threw his head back, and began to laugh hysterically. A neighbor of the **Alatandos, Alfonso**, recognized Clemente by his bright red hair and green, canvas clothing. He had seen the hunchback scraping along the street only a few minutes earlier.

"Clemente! Is that you?"

Clemente was still laughing, eyes shut, and holding his side. Without looking to see who'd asked the question, he said, "Yes! And I'm on my feet! A monk did this to me."

"It's a miracle! A miracle!" Alfonso began shouting. And a small crowd began to gather. "Does your mother know of this?"

Clemente stopped laughing. He thought of his mama. "No," he answered solemnly. "I must see her right away."

"I will walk with you," said Alfonso.

The small crowd around Clemente had begun to attract attention on the normally quiet street. People began coming out of their homes. "What is all the fuss?"

"They say it is the hunchback boy. That is him walking ahead!"

"I would not have recognized him."

"I hear a monk cured him ...They say it is a miracle!"

"What monk?"

"I do not know, let's follow him and find out."

By the time Clemente reached the front of his little home, more than forty villagers encircled him. His mother came to the door to see what the commotion was about. "What's going on?" she asked.

The crowd was facing her, and all conversation ceased. They were all anxious to hear her reaction. Clemente stepped to the front and smiled at his mother. Her eyes passed him over. "What is the trouble?" she demanded. "Has something happened to my son? Please, tell me he is alright!"

Clemente stepped forward a few more paces. "Mama... Do you not recognize your own son?"

She stared at Clemente and began to tremble. He began moving slowly towards her, taking small steps. She outstretched her arms and leaped forward, embracing him. Both were in tears.

The crowd began to buzz again. "Tell us what happened, Clemente... Did you say a monk did this wonder?"

"Y-Yes…"

His mother was stroking his hair when she noticed his shirt.

"Clemente-Are you all right? Look ... You are bleeding." Clemente looked down at the blood on the shoulder of his shirt. "No, that is not my blood, Mama. That is where the monk touched me. I remember now. His hands were bleeding!"

"It was Padre Pio!" shouted Alfonso, who had been standing close enough to hear the conversation. "He says the monk had bleeding hands!"

The crowd became excited. His mother said, "Son, we must go up to the monastery and see if it was Padre Pio that you saw. If it is, we must get down on our knees and thank him!"

Over a hundred persons joined Clemente and his mother on their climb to the monastery. Alfonso tugged on the rope which rang the inside bell. Brother Gaudenzio opened the door.

"We want to see Padre Pio," Alfonso said enthusiastically. "Today he was in town and cured my neighbor, Clemente. It's a miracle!"

Brother Gaudenzio was confused. "I am sorry, my friend, but Padre Pio has not left here since the day he first arrived. You must be mistaken."

Clemente stepped forward. "Please. A monk with bleeding hands has given me a new life. May I at least see Pio?"

Brother Gaudenzio hesitated for a moment, then agreed to ask Padre Pio to see them. He shut the door, but returned a few minutes later with Pio at his side. Clemente recognized Pio immediately. "It is him, Mama." Clemente dropped to his knees before the priest, kissing his hand.

"You should be kissing the hand of your mother, Clemente." Pio spoke gently. "It was her prayers that God heard."

"But Padre ... it was you that I…"

"Hush." Pio smiled at him.

"Give us your blessings, Padre," came a voice from the rear of the crowd. The villagers kneeled, and Pio made the sign of the cross over them. Then they began to throw questions at him, but he did not respond. Instead, he turned around in the doorway and disappeared. Brother Gaudenzio followed, closing the door behind him. "Padre Pio," called Gaudenzio in the corridor. "Surely the boy must be mistaken ... You have never left this place."

Pio responded only with a mumble.

Chapter 35

Church reactions to reports of the stigmata were not forthcoming, at least not official reactions. Unofficially, there was great polarization. There were priests and church superiors the world over who were extremely vocal over the events at San Giovanni Rotondo. Some supported Padre Pio on blind faith. Others took the opposite extreme and condemned him as a charlatan. The press sensationalized the rumors that spread and printed them as official releases from San Giovanni. The continued silence of the official voice of the Church gave credence to the lies in the media by not refuting them.

In her effort to reduce the rumors about Padre Pio, the Church did act, though it may have been a wrong reaction. The Church decreed that Padre Pio refrain from having any contact with his parishioners. This was a terrible blow to those who needed him. Worse, it made Padre Pio a prisoner in the cloister. Most of the day, while people entered the grounds for services and other business, it confined the friar-priest to his cell. He had to avoid his beloved chapel during all public services. He could not attend Mass. It was one of the most trying times of his life.

The wisdom of the Church dates back almost two millennia. She knows that all is not as it always seems. People are an emotional lot. They are easily caught up in causes that are not what they seem. Throughout the world events take place frequently that are unexplainable, that appear supernatural, miraculous. The Church cannot investigate everyone. Only if there is merit will she get involved.

In Padre Pio's case, **The Vatican** became involved by having the Holy Office look into the matter. At the beginning of the investigation, the Holy Office restricted Padre Pio from offering Mass in public. The action brought about a demonstration from almost all of the three thousand residents of San Giovanni Rotondo. A petition was sent to Rome, and after two weeks the decree was suspended.

Toward the end of 1919 rumors began to spread that Padre Pio was to be moved from San Giovanni. Again demonstrations began, and those rumors disappeared. Throughout this time the number of pilgrims coming to the small town increased by the week. The pilgrims brought a new wealth to the town, but they also brought problems. Now there were almost as many visitors as residents at any one time. With the restrictions on Padre Pio's time and the competition from outsiders for the few hours he could spend with his flock each week, some of the people became envious of every moment their shepherd had for the people. All this added to the polarization that now surrounded every aspect of the friar's life.

A delicate status quo seemed to prevail for about another year, through most of 1920.

Chapter 36

Victoro continued his carousing. He sold his cobbler shop leaving the old widow without any income. That didn't concern him. He took a room at the inn across the road from the tavern at the edge of town. With part of the money he received from the sale of the shop he purchased an interest in the tavern. Now his charisma attracted new customers to the place, and it afforded him a better income than the cobbler shop had.

He never returned to his mother's home. He sent a customer to pick up his belongings. On a few occasions he passed the woman on the street with not so much as a greeting. The girl who was to have been his bride now only remained in his memory as someone he occasionally lusted for.

Over the next year, Victoro's activities were so outrageous that no one from his past had anything to do with him. Only his mother and Padre Pio even cared what happened to him. They were the only two who seemed to understand what had happened, and they made no effort to explain it to anyone. It was as if both were waiting, waiting for something else to evolve in this mystery that was Victoro.

During the night of October 13, 1920, Victoro had a dream. In that dream a demon set before Victoro a large tray that contained on it a feast. As Victoro approached the banquet he recognized that what had looked like delicacies of all varieties were really not foods at all. Each morsel in turn changed into a scene of his activities since that day he failed to appear at Mass or at his cobbler shop. His new life was unfolding before his eyes. Each outrage and sin in turn was being reviewed before him upon that tray, which was now like a golden stage.

As he watched himself drinking, partying, fornicating, gorging, he realized that he had broken every commandment save one. As he watched he savored and enjoyed each excessive act more than when it originally took place.

In the morning of October 14, 1920, Victoro awoke early, just before dawn. He could feel he had a mission that day, though he knew not yet what it was. He dressed quickly and was out on the street in the first sunlight. He wandered aimlessly between the inn and the tavern and up and down the dirt road that ran between the two. At last he saw another person coming up the road from the countryside. Victoro felt compelled to give that person a message and started toward him, not knowing what that message even was.

"Hold there friend," he said to the stranger, not knowing what his next words would be but confident the words would come. "I have disturbing news for all who live in and about San Giovanni. Today a letter arrives at the monastery ordering that our Padre Pio be sent away forever. We must not let that happen. Gather all your friends and weapons and meet at the square at ten. Spread the word rapidly."

There was such conviction and urgency in Victoro's words that the stranger didn't even question how he knew of the letter. Had he asked, Victoro could not have answered him, but Victoro in his own mind knew without a doubt that he spoke fact and that his was the only action to be taken.

All through the early morning Victoro spread his message, and reaction was almost universal. People all over the town gathered their friends and persuaded them to respond. At ten o'clock the town square was filled. Most of the people carried weapons, pitchforks, kitchen knives, clubs, rifles, pistols, and bayonets they had smuggled home with them from the war.

Victoro was waiting for them. He stood on a platform in the square from which he would make a speech. He had no idea what his speech would be about, but again he was confident that at the proper time the right words would come.

Not everyone in the square that morning was prepared to follow Victoro on his mission. As the message spread through the town earlier, there were those who felt that if the Church felt Padre Pio should be moved, then that was what should be done. These faithful were indeed a minority, but they were there to espouse and defend their position ... to defend the position of the Church.

At about ten after ten Victoro raised his arms for silence. "My friends, fellow citizens of San Giovanni Rotondo. Today they plan to take our Padre Pio from our midst. Not just for a while, but forever. We must not let that happen. What's worse, they wish to take him to Spain ... out of Italy altogether. We must not let that happen.

"All the world will think we in San Giovanni Rotondo do not believe in or love our Padre Pio. All the world will think all of Italy does not believe in or love Padre Pio.

"We must do all in our power to keep Padre Pio with us. We must let no one in to the monastery who is not one of us. Strangers must be kept from his door."

A man who had worked his way near to the platform from which Victoro spoke, called out, "How is it that you know of the letter and its contents? How do you come to the authority to speak against the will of the Church?"

Victoro didn't even try to answer. He merely pointed at him and spoke to the crowd. "He is one who wants to take our Padre Pio from our midst. He is one of those who must be silenced." The crowd turned against the man. Some of his friends tried to get to his aid. A riot broke out. Screams, profanities, shots echoed in the square. On October 14, 1920, fourteen people died in the riot that broke out in the square in San Giovanni Rotondo.

By the time word got to the monastery of the events down the mountain it was all over. Again Padre Pio seemed to be aware of the events before the news got to him. "There are things in which we are helpless to intervene. They are preordained by higher powers and we must stand by and watch them take their course." Tears welled in his eyes. The cloister remained locked that day. Padre Pio knelt before the cross in his cell and prayed for the fourteen souls and for the soul of his friend Victoro.

Later that day, a communiqué came to the office of the Provincial Father in Foggia. It was from the Holy Office, suggesting that Padre Pio be moved from his residence at San Giovanni Rotondo. Because of the tragic riot that order was rescinded.

Chapter 37

After the bloody riot of October 14, 1920, the Church withdrew any plan to move Padre Pio from the monastery at San Giovanni Rotondo, but with that decision came another edict that restricted his activities mercilessly. In this instance it seemed the Church had allied herself with the devil to prevent Padre Pio from doing God's work.

In August of 1923 there was again an order to move Padre Pio, but somehow the townspeople found out about that plot also, and in fear of another disastrous riot that order was suspended on August 17, 1923.

If the Vatican thought the world would forget about Padre Pio by keeping him from having contact with the people; the Vatican was wrong. The people of San Giovanni demonstrated continuously for more contact with their beloved Capuchin. An increasing number of pilgrims made their way to the little town. Gradually the Provincial Father allowed the friar-priest to in crease his activities on a very limited basis. That settled down the demonstrations a little. But the more Padre Pio worked with the people, the more wondrous were reports of him. The Church could not keep him a secret. He was a growing legend. In April of 1931, the Church once more began talk of moving him from the town that loved him.

On the night of April 7, 1931, Victoro again had a dream. Over the years he continued to live at the inn, which he now owned. The original owner had died, and Victoro had taken up with the man's widow. He had persuaded her to sign over all her holdings to him with a promise to marry her. He did not keep his part of the bargain, and she committed suicide, leaving him undisputed owner. The tavern was now all his. He acquired his partner's share by buying back his gambling losses and other debts at a fraction of their worth, after he persuaded the creditors that the man had no hope of paying them anything at all.

Victoro's mother was now aged but was in remarkably good health. All the town admired her for the way she stood up to her ordeal. In spite of her son's considerable wealth, he offered in no way to help her. It is doubtful that she would have accepted any help from him under the circumstances. Her only help came from Padre Pio's visitations and God. "Have faith that God has not forsaken your son. He is now upon an unholy mission not of his own choosing. When the devil forsakes him, as he surely will, our Lord will be ready to have him back among us," Padre Pio would reassure the woman when her grief would cry out over the monastery walls to him.

When Victoro awoke on the morning of April 8, he was again driven by an energy he didn't understand. Again he gathered a crowd with news of plans to whisk away their friar-priest. When most of the townspeople had gathered in the square, he began to speak words that sounded like his own, but which were from another intelligence: "Again the Church superiors threaten to take away our Padre Pio. How often are we to be trifled with like this? We must put an end to this once and for all.

"At this very moment there is a visiting priest at the monastery. I'll wager he is preparing to transfer our sainted priest. My friends, Padre Pio is the life and spirit of our town. The pilgrimages bring us much needed business. Our town is blessed to have our Padre Pio. We have wasted too much time already with idle talk. It is time that we storm that fortress and settle the matter forever."

One of the crowd asked, "And if we storm the monastery, what then?"

"Leave that to me," Victoro replied. "We must see to it that the visitor goes, without our Padre Pio. We must keep our saint" here at all costs. Dead or alive, Padre Pio must stay here!"

A silence fell over the crowd, but no one spoke against the idea. "Think," Victoro continued, "A saint is a saint, dead or alive. He is our 'saint'. If they will not let him live with us, then perhaps they will let him be at his eternal rest with us. At least then there would be no further threats to steal him away." Victoro paused for a moment and then commanded, "Now let's waste no more time. To the monastery…let no one turn his back."

If anyone had wanted to speak out against Victoro in the square that day, he must have remembered what happened to the dissenter years before. The mob turned from the square and massed toward the road up to the cloister.

When the mob reached the monastery it did not stop. The people didn't pull at the rope that rang the bell to summon the friars. They broke down the door and swarmed through the high walls. Both men and women surged into the off limits areas. Women, who were at risk of excommunication for violation of a monastic enclosure gave no second thought to what they were doing. There was "an enemy in the fortress" intent on taking away their 'saint', and they were going to have that foe.

Padre Raffaele, the new **Superior of the Monastery**, tried to pacify the mob. He met them at the head of a stairway and barely got them stopped long enough to listen. Yes, there was a visiting priest in the friary. No, he was not there to whisk away Padre Pio. Yes, they had heard that the Holy Office was again thinking of transferring Padre Pio, but no, there had not been any orders yet to implement any move.

"We do not believe you," Victoro spoke for the mob.

"It is so. The visiting priest is in transit. He has nothing to do with Padre Pio's future."

Victoro did not want the superior to sway his followers, and he spoke haltingly. "You say that under obedience to the Church. We do not believe what you tell us. You are lying!"

"I am a son of Saint Francis," the superior responded, anger showing in his own voice now. "I am not given to lying. We are Capuchin Brothers and will give hospitality to any priest we choose at any time we choose. The priest is scheduled to leave tomorrow. He will be allowed to stay. It is not a matter of your jurisdiction. When he leaves tomorrow he will leave alone as he came."

If the superior intimidated the mob with his tone, he made no impression on Victoro. Again Victoro accused the superior of being not totally honest with them. "Bring us Padre Pio. If he tells us, we will believe him."

The superior hesitated, and then thought that it would be the only way to disperse the mob. "Very well. Wait here, I will bring him to you."

As brother Raffaele turned to get Padre Pio, he didn't notice that Victoro whispered something into the ear of one of his cronies. The man to whom Victoro whispered was a ruffian who was in trouble most of the time, not because of meanness, but because of dullness. He'd always been slow, and considered a moron by most of the townspeople. As a child he always took dares. It was the only way he got attention and acceptance. As he grew older, people took advantage of him by getting him to do tasks that were either too dangerous or too illegal for intelligent people to risk. Victoro was quick to take advantage of this buffoon over the years. As he whispered to him now, an expression of self-importance came over the ruffian's face.

Moments later, Brother Raffaele returned with Padre Pio; as quickly as he appeared the tension left the mob. In an instant they were a controllable crowd. Padre Pio spoke to them, reassured them, advised them to go back down to San Giovanni Rotondo and attend to their business. No one noticed that Victoro's ruffian was working his way to the edge of the crowd nearest where Padre Pio stood. Suddenly he lunged toward Padre Pio, a revolver drawn. Everyone stood'aghast at the sight of the man pointing a pistol at Padre Pio's head. It was one thing to consider such an act while standing a mile-and-a-half away in the town square; it was quite another thing to see a beloved friend's life threatened. Only Victoro stood expectantly wide eyed. He said nothing. Let the boob take full credit for this act.

"You will stay with us forever, Padre Pio," the pawn stammered. "Dead or alive, you'll never leave this village."

Padre Pio remained remarkably calm. Turning directly into the gun he stared at it only a second, then into the eyes of the gunman. He smiled at him compassionately and held out his hand to the man. He didn't say a word, but it was as if they were having a silent conversation. Tears came to the gunman's eyes, and he fell to his knees before his victim. Padre Pio took the gun from his hand and blessed him. The crowd watched silently, then one or two went to their knees to pray, then the rest. Victoro had worked his way to the back of the crowd. No one noticed as he let himself out the broken down door in frustration. He thought as he went, *I'm not through with you yet, Padre Pio.*

Chapter 38

In June of 1931, Gena came to San Giovanni Rotondo on a pilgrimage. She was three months widowed. Because of serious financial problems her three children were living with their paternal grandparents. The first place she saw as she came to San Giovanni Rotondo was Victoro's inn. She didn't know whether she could afford lodging there, but she needed a place to stay and thought she would at least ask about the rates. Victoro happened to be at the desk, and when he saw the single woman come in he decided he would like to have her stay. From her appearance he could tell she was not a woman of means. He quoted her a very attractive price, and she took a room.

After the events of April 8, the Holy Office of the Church in Rome dismissed any ideas of transferring Padre Pio. Instead they reacted by cutting him off from any public contact. The restrictions were the most severe ever imposed on the churchman. On June 9, a letter arrived from the Vatican. Its instructions were explicit: "Padre Pio, Capuchin friar-priest of San Giovanni Rotondo and from Pietrelcina, is to desist from all activity except the celebration of Mass when only servers are present. He is to be forbidden all contact with seculars. He is to be restricted to his own cell except for a strict schedule: He shall be allowed two hours in the morning for Mass. He may go to prayers in the oratory until noon. He may take to the library one hour each day for study. He may go to prayer in the afternoon after Vespers and then may go to prayer until midnight. He is deprived of all his priestly powers except for the right to celebrate Mass when no persons other than Brothers are present."

It was a severe blow to the priest. When the restrictions were read to him, tears welled up in his eyes. "If I am ordered, so I will bear this imprisonment of my soul and my body. Let God's will be done."

As soon as Gena settled into her room in Victoro's inn she started up the mountain to the monastery. She arrived there tired but eager to see her Padre Pio. She had planned this pilgrimage for some time, even before her husband died. Over the years she had wanted to thank Padre Pio for saving her from evil. Now that her husband had died she felt the need to see him even more, not only to thank him, but to pray with him and ask him to hear her confession. She arrived at the church of Saint Mary of the Graces just to find out that Padre Pio was not allowed to see anyone. She prayed alone and thanked him in her prayers. She made her confession to another of the friar-priests and then returned to the inn. When she entered her disappointment was evident. Victoro took the opportunity to speak to her.

"My but you look unhappy. Did your journey go poorly?"

"My journey was fine, but I was unable to see Padre Pio."

"He isn't ill, I hope."

"I don't think so. I was told that he is not presently serving his flock."

"Well, perhaps tomorrow then."

"No, I asked. I was told that his leave of duties is for an indefinite period of time. I did so want to see him. My heart begs to see him."

"Don't despair. It is probably just temporary. Stay a few days and then try again. You will see."

"Oh, if only I could, but I can't afford such extravagance. I've limited funds, only enough for another day or two if I'm careful."

"My dear, I can see how much this means to you. Let me help you. I'll find you a less expensive room, and I'll not charge you. You can take your meals here also, and I'll throw them into the bargain." ·

"Oh, I couldn't. That's too generous of you. It is none of your concern. But I do thank you for the offer."

"I insist. It will only be for a few days, I'm sure. Please let me do this. It isn't too often that a man in my business gets an opportunity to do a good deed. I beg you, do me the honor of being my guest. After all, how often will you have a chance to get back here to see Padre Pio? I do it for him, too."

His power of persuasion was too great for her. She finally agreed to accept his hospitality. He had her move to a room he said was less in demand than the one she'd originally gotten. It was next to his own suite.

Tired from her long pilgrimage and her disappointing climb to the monastery, Gena excused herself to bathe and rest before she could even think about dinner. "I insist that you dine with me tonight," Victoro said as he left her at her room, and before he departed she agreed.

In the years since Padre Pio exorcised her, Gena was no more a victim of the devil's possession, but she was still human and subject to human needs. Though she grieved for her husband, she was desperately lonely, especially since her children went to live with her in-laws. Victoro was one of the few people with whom she'd spoken in many months and certainly the first single man.

The room was small and rustic, with a single window that looked out from the side of the inn to some fields. It was quiet, and quite clean. She was surprised to see how large the bed was. The linens were fresh and the mattress was not straw-filled. The pillows, there were two of them, were feather-filled. Along one wall was a small dresser, and on it was a large washbowl and a large pitcher filled with water for bathing. Next to it was the largest mirror she'd ever seen; big enough to reflect the whole room. On the wall opposite the window hung a picture, and above it there was a ventilator of some kind, covered by a grate.

Gena unpacked her few belongings and placed them in the dresser. Then she poured some of the water into the washbowl. She found a washcloth and a large towel in the dresser. She began to undress.

At first something disturbed her. Then she realized it was the mirror. She'd never seen herself in a mirror that showed her entire body from head to foot. And she'd never undressed where she could watch herself. It's like someone being in the room with me. She chuckled at her own silliness and continued to disrobe.

Once undressed, she was almost fascinated by her own nakedness. She realized she'd never seen herself like this. The only mirror she'd ever had was barely large enough to comb her hair by. She found herself staring at the image. She was surprised, pleased, at how good she still looked. Though she'd nursed three babies, her breasts were still firm, well shaped, full, and not at all pendulous like those of most women her age. Despite three pregnancies, her stomach was quite flat, well muscled, the skin still soft and smooth, without the telltale stretch marks that so many women have. She felt ashamed that she stared at herself so long. She took the washcloth, put it in the water, and soaped it. She began to wash, almost as a distraction, but even then she could not take her eyes off of the naked image.

She continued to wash, turning her back to the mirror. I'll not give in to this temptation. Yet I still feel I'm being watched. She could see the room was empty. I feel as though I'm on display. She was compelled to turn again, to see whether the image in the mirror was still watching her.

Victoro's bedroom was next to hers. In it he had built a closet. When its door was kept closed it would have been dark inside, like any other closet, except for the light that was admitted through the ventilator grate Victoro placed in its back wall. That ventilator opened into Gena's room and allowed Victoro to take pleasure in spying on whatever went on in that room. He rented the room to attractive women, or couples he thought might have interesting relationships, and frequently allowed the tavern girls to take their clientele there. He especially liked renting that room to women he suspected of being lesbians. He found watching those couples most erotic of all.

Gena's eyes were again captured by the image in the mirror. *How strange… when I was twelve I looked eighteen, now that I am thirty-eight, I look to be in my very early thirties. Time has always been kind to me, at least in my later years.* She looked at her face. *The gray is hardly noticeable.* She reached up and pulled out the two most obvious strands. The hair hung almost to her shoulders, soft, smooth, still beautiful, deep red. There was still fire in her eyes. Even through her fatigue they danced with youth. Her cheeks had good color, and her skin was younger than her years. *Thank God, I've been spared fieldwork. My skin's been kept from the drying sun.*

Her eyes followed down to her neck and body as she sponged away the soap with a cloth she'd dipped in the fresh water left in the pitcher. She sponged off her shoulders and then her breasts. She felt some of the excess water run down her body and quickly she laid the towel on the floor and stepped on it. She wrung out the washcloth a little to control the runoff a little better. The cooling water felt good on her breasts. She had always been sensitive there. As she continued to wash the breasts she noticed a blush on her upper chest, an inner warmth she always felt when she started to get aroused. Her nipples began to erect. *Oh my ... I haven't felt this since ...* her thoughts drifted to her dead husband. *Tony, why did you have to die? They were such good years we had.* Tears began to form in her eyes. *I want you now, Tony. Is it you who makes me feel I'm being watched? Are you with me, Tony?* With that thought the sensation of being seen in her bath added to her erotic feelings, as when she tried to entice him, when her passions occasionally aroused first. "Gena, you always have been too hot-blooded for your own good," she mouthed toward the image in the mirror.

She dipped the cloth into the fresh water again, wrung it, and went on to sponge her tummy. The excitement remained with her. She washed downward. Her eyes continued down. She realized that in nearly forty years she'd never really seen her whole body ... not as he'd seen it.

She studied herself. She looked up at the hair on her head, then back down again. *The hair is darker below…I've never noticed that before. I've never seen myself, all, like this.* She sponged over the pubis. Again the cool cloth aroused her feelings. *Oh, Tony, I need you now. It's been so long. Too long.* She lingered there a moment with the sponge, then pulled away.

"No," she uttered, "I'll not give in to it." She quickly dipped the cloth and without wringing it out sponged her legs down. "I'll not give in to my passions." She picked up the towel and patted herself dry. She wrapped herself in the towel and went to the bed, drew back the cover, and lay down. The amorous feelings would not leave. The more she tried to get them off her mind, the stronger they grew. *Oh, Tony, why did you leave? It was so wonderful with you.* Her hand moved down on her body, over the flat, smooth stomach. She hesitated, frowned a moment, then with a sigh of resignation let her fingers run through the tangle of moist, cool, curls of hair. "Oh, it's been such a long time. I can't help myself, Tony." She climaxed quickly and fell off into a deep sleep.

In the small closet on the other side of the ventilator grate, Victoro, too, was fondling the evidence of his excitement.

Chapter 39

The Church's investigation of Padre Pio was an ongoing process. It had begun with the appearance of the stigmata, and had not ceased in all the years since. Numerous investigators were involved with Padre Pio's case over the years. One who had followed it, and had been included in the investigations since their inception, was **Father Mario de Sica**. He had been assigned to the Holy Office of the Vatican almost since his ordination. A fine scholar and researcher, his talents lent themselves especially to this work of the Holy Office. He knew perhaps as much about Padre Pio as any man outside of the friary at San Giovanni Rotondo. All studies, examinations, testimonies, and correspondence were available to him as they came to the Vatican. He'd made exhaustive studies himself, having letters and articles from newspapers and magazines forwarded to him from all over the world. He also knew most of the wildest rumors.

Father Mario was a pious man. His faith and devotion were unquestioned. His religion was a very personal thing to him, and he didn't mind not having a parish or dealing with the public. That made him no less devout a priest. It was his own religious zeal that kept him skeptical of all the claims about Padre Pio. He could not understand why God would have chosen a Capuchin friar priest for such a saintly event as the stigmata. No doubt Padre Pio was pious. There was no question that he had studied hard. No one questioned his selfless service. But there were thousands of priests with better background and heritage, better educated and longer in service to mankind, who seemed more likely chosen if God needed an emissary here on earth.

Some of the stories, especially those from media, and many from rumor or claims of individual people who said they had holy encounters with Padre Pio, he considered preposterous, and rightly so. Padre Pio and his staunchest supporters would have disclaimed them also. But there were many incidents that appeared to be so well documented that Father Mario remained doubtful of; it was his job to remain doubtful, to question every claim, regardless of its seeming authenticity, regardless of the stature of the personage giving testimony. It was his place to throw cold water on any overly enthusiastic support for the Capuchin. His position was to remain absolutely objective in evaluation of all matters concerning Padre Pio. Of course, everything he knew about the friar was from what he'd read or heard. Most of those reports came from the areas of San Giovanni Rotondo and Pietrelcina. "Those people have much to gain by having a saint in their midst," he often said. "Their claims would likely become embellished. I'm certain many are figments of over-active imaginations."

Over the years, Father Mario became more skeptical.

Chapter 40

The sun had already set when a knock came at Gena's door. She awoke confused. She was naked in a strange bed, in a strange room. The moon dimly lit the chamber, not enough to let her get her bearings. The knock came a second time, and with it the first familiar environ, the voice of Victoro. "Gena! Wake up Gena! You've slept three hours already. Wake up and have some dinner. You can return to your bed after you've eaten."

Gena reoriented and replied to Victoro's invitation. "I'll be down in just a few moments. I just have to get dressed." She groped in the darkness. She found the kerosene lamp that stood on the vanity next to the washbasin, but she couldn't find the matches for a few moments. Finally, she accidentally swept them off the vanity and heard them fall to the floor. She groped a few seconds more, where she heard them strike the floor. Picking them up she went first to the window and drew a shade. Then she struck a match and lit the lamp. The room brightened only a little, but at least she could find her clothes. She caught another glimpse of herself in the mirror and remembered. It made her feel a little ashamed, and she turned quickly away not to be reminded.

Victoro waited downstairs. He was behind the desk checking through his ledger when he saw her come down. Seeing her rekindled some of the feelings he'd had earlier that afternoon. "Well, you've had quite a nap. You seem quite refreshed."

I've got to have you, He was thinking.

"Yes, I didn't mean to sleep so long. I hardly ever take a nap. I guess I was more tired than I thought."

"It's too late to eat here tonight. My cook's gone home. I thought it more important to let you rest and decided to take you out to a little place just a short way up the road. It's a nice moonlit night. We can walk."

"It's really not necessary. I'm not that hungry. I don't want to put you to any trouble."

"It's not a question of trouble. I'm starved, and I hate to eat alone. You'll be doing me a great favor to join me. Besides, you've already given your promise." *I'll have you soon,* he reflected.

The evening was cool, there were only a few clouds in the sky. "No need to worry about rain tonight," Victoro commented.

"It's a lovely night for walking," Gena replied. When they got to the restaurant Gena realized that she was hungrier than she'd earlier believed. They both ate heartily, and she drank a little more wine than she'd intended. Victoro was as charming as he could be when he wanted. She talked freely of her past, of her children, her life with Tony. She explained how her husband had died during the flu epidemic. By the time they'd finished eating he knew all about her, and she knew only what he wanted her to know about him. She found him very likable, attractive. He made her laugh and feel as she'd not felt since Tony courted her so many years ago. She wished the evening wouldn't end.

She was surprised when the proprietor came to the table and announced, "I'm sorry, it is our closing time, past eleven." He looked nervously at Victoro, fearing the man might explode, as was his reputation when someone interfered with his entertainment. To the host's relief, Victoro continued to play the role of a charming person. Besides, he was hoping to spend more time with Gena back at the inn, perhaps in his or her quarters.

"I'm sorry friend. I had no idea it was already so late. Time flies when you're with such lovely company."

When they got up to leave, Gena felt a little wobbly on her feet, giddy from the wine. "Oh my, I think I may have had a bit too much to drink."

Victoro laughed politely and offered her his arm to stabilize her. By the time they got outside he had his arm around her waist, and she was leaning against him, comfortable, secure in his firm grasp.

"This fresh air will help, but if the wine makes you feel happy and relaxed it's better to stay that way." He hoped she would not recover too quickly and hurried her back to the inn.

"Would you like to come to my room? We could continue our conversation there. I'm not ready for the evening to end yet," Victoro said.

"I really shouldn't. It doesn't seem right."

"Nonsense, this is 1931, not the Middle Ages. Besides, we're beyond that. Neither of us are children. There wouldn't even be anyone to gossip, and I assure you nothing will happen against your will."

It is my will I'm afraid of, Gena thought. She hesitated.

"Please, trust me. It's so early, and you did have a long nap today."

She was persuaded. "For just a little while. Please don't think I do this often."

"I'm sure this is a first," he reassured her.

Victoro's suite was large and lavishly furnished. Gena had never seen such opulence outside of magazine pictures. Woolen oriental carpeting lay on the floors. Heavy velvet drapes framed the windows. The furniture was heavy, polished wood and the finest upholstery. A large tapestry hung on the wall behind a luxurious, large sofa. There was statuary, mostly of nude women. She immediately noticed that there were electric lights, not the kerosene lamps that left a petroleum odor and dim light throughout the rest of the inn. There were several paintings about the room, all of nudes.

"Make yourself comfortable, please," Victoro said, offering her the sofa. He purposely did not sit down next to her but drew up a chair across a small table from her.

"It's a lovely place you have here."

"Thank you. I'm glad you like it. It's taken me years to get it just the way I want it." He continued talking as he got up and brought a bottle of wine from a cabinet. "I'm terribly thirsty. Won't you join me in a glass of wine?"

"I really shouldn't. I already drank too much, and I still feel it from dinner."

"One more won't hurt. Besides, it'll make you sleep better."

"Oh, I think I'll sleep well. I'm still tired, even with the nap I had today. I guess the trip was really exhausting. But I will have one glass with you. You've been so kind to me. I can't remember when I've been treated so wonderfully. You're really a very nice man."

"Nonsense," Victoro said as he poured the wine, "I've only done what anyone else would have done for you."

They talked on and Victoro kept pouring wine into Gena's glass, never letting it empty. She had no idea of how much she drank. She talked and laughed, became giddier, and then a bit dizzy. "Oh my, I think I'm getting drunk. Now what will you think of me?"

"I think you're wonderful. So what if you are a little tipsy?" Again he filled her glass. But he'd miscalculated. She'd already had too much.

"Oh my, I know I've had too much. I'd better go to my room while I still can," and without waiting for his response she got up and started for the door. She faltered and he grabbed for her.

"Here, let me help you."

"Oh, I'm sorry. I feel so foolish. I must go while I still can." She wobbled toward the door and again he had to stabilize her walking. He wanted to take the bottle and glasses with him, but she moved too fast and gave him no opportunity to do anything but help her walk and open the doors for her. When they got to her room he sat her on the edge of her bed. She fell over backwards, unconscious.

Victoro tried to wake her, but she was not to be roused. He lifted her on to the bed properly, and she didn't stir. It irritated him. He'd had such erotic visions of his night with her. He remembered what he'd watched through the ventilator, and it frustrated him even more, now she was drunk into unconsciousness.

Shit! I guess I might as well leave her like that all night. I could have a maid undress her and put her under her covers. Then a gleam came to his eyes. He recalled her nakedness. He wanted to see her that way again. Perhaps he could. He went back to the door to the hall and closed it, locked it. Again he tried to rouse her. *She'll not awaken for hours. She'll never know.*

Excitement coursed through his body. This would be a new experience for him. He planned how to do this so he would get the most pleasure, to savor its delights. He removed her shoes and her stockings. Her feet were small, almost dainty. He looked at her face. She was oblivious to what was going on. He loosened her belt and unbuttoned her blouse. He had to raise her up to slip it off. She wore only a slip under it, and he felt her firm breasts through the fabric. She didn't stir. Now he pulled her skirt down and off. Reaching up under her slip he felt for her undergarment. He felt her through it before slipping it off. She slept only in her slip. He wanted her desperately. *What if she wakes up? But she won't. She hasn't moved a muscle through all of this. She'll never know. And if she does awaken, I'll just convince her she submitted before passing out.*

He chuckled and removed the slip. He felt all over her body to heighten his excitement. He kissed her everywhere. He'd always taken pleasure in the fervor of the women he made love to. He'd always thought that it would be no great pleasure to have sex with a woman who didn't respond, but this was extremely erotic to him, like stealing and voyeuring at the same time. He could stand no more. He kicked off his shoes and dropped his trousers and shorts.

It was difficult penetrating her without her help, but that only excited him more. At last he accomplished full insertion. She slept on. She was limp under him. Sleep tightly my dear, don't let me disturb you. This is better than I'd hope for. He thrust deep and she moaned a little. Again he thrust, again and again ...and then he was through.

Victoro dressed. He cleaned her as well as he could. He folded her clothes as neatly as he could and put them in a drawer. He turned down the kerosene lamp. She slept on. He covered her and let himself out of the room.

Chapter 41

"But Doctor, how can you classify Clemente's case as a miracle? According to your X rays, the lungs and heart are still arched like that of a hunchback. Only the spine is straight. If it were in fact a miraculous cure, wouldn't the organs also be in their proper positions?" Father Mario was slouched back in the worn wing chair, rubbing his temples. He was becoming very disgruntled at what he thought to be a very narrow-minded diagnosis from **Dr. Pullo**.

When Father Mario first approached him for an interview, Dr. Pullo felt flattered to be of assistance to an emissary from the Holy City. He thought that he would have an important role in helping the Church establish credibility to the miracle. But now he was beginning to question the intentions of his guest. "Father," he began, "I delivered Clemente into this world-with my own hands, a hunchback. Now his spine is straighter than yours or mine. He stands on two feet for the first time since his birth. This, in itself, can only be described as a miracle!"

"Doctor, I am asking you if there have been known cases of spines such as Clemente's righting themselves through time or, maybe, a freakish accident. I'm sure that…"

"I have patients to attend to, Father," snapped Dr. Pullo. "I have told you all I possibly can."

Father Mario could see that he was getting nowhere. *To question the doctor any further would be futile. He's as fanatical as the rest.*

"Would you like a copy of my report, Father?"

"That won't be necessary."

"Then I bid you good-day."

Chapter 42

If Victoro and the devil were happy over the severe restrictions placed on Padre Pio by the Church, they were not alone. Father Mario de Sica was also more than pleased. Over the years he had been gladdened each time the Church decided to restrict the friar; had been increasingly frustrated each time the restrictions had been rescinded.

He fully agreed with the "wisdom" of the Church when Padre Pio's superiors restricted his priestly activities in 1920. It disturbed him greatly that **Pope Benedictus XV** espoused, the renowned Capuchin almost from the time of the appearance of the stigmata. He felt gratified when Pope Pius XI, who took over after the death of Pope Benedictus XV on January 22, 1922, reacted to the opposition to the friar by restricting his activities further.

He felt devastated when, in 1929, Pope Pius XI had a change of heart, in consideration of many of the well documented miracles involving the Capuchin, and lifted many of the restrictions on July 28, 1929. And, though he was distressed at the bloodshed of the riots and the demonstrations of the people of San Giovanni Rotondo, he was delighted that the Church again responded to those events by placing the severest restrictions ever on Padre Pio in her decree of June 9, 1931.

Now he felt it his personal mission to see that those restrictions would never be lifted again.

Chapter 43

From the window of his cell, Padre Pio could look out over the great wall of the friary. From his vantage he could see down onto the town of San Giovanni Rotondo, the last part of the mountain road that led up to the cloister. The view was beautiful but painful. It deepened his suffering to be able to see the townspeople and pilgrims climbing the steep grade to Saint Mary of the Graces, knowing that he was not allowed to serve them.

A breeze from the garden carried the sweet aroma of flowers to the Capuchin. He looked up at the blue, cloudless sky. It was indeed a wonderful day, but Padre Pio was disturbed. By whatever way knowledge came to him of the outside world, he knew of Gena's unsuccessful effort to see him. He knew of her encounter with Victoro. Though no one else but Victoro, not even Gena herself, knew of the sinful event of the previous night, Padre Pio knew of the devilish act. *How, my Heavenly Father am I to help her? How am I to protect her? What is Your purpose?* He received no answer, no guidance. *If it is Your will, Father, I bear it gladly; but if only I could understand…*

As he prayed, he became aware of a putrid odor replacing the fragrance of the garden. He frowned and mouthed, "You are here, my old enemy."

Within the hour Padre Pio developed a high fever. He began a fast.

Over the years he'd continued having occasional nighttime duels with demons. They were not as violent as those he'd had in Pietrelcina, but the sound that came from his cell at those times were hideous. The other friars were at first terrified by the struggles, but like the people of Pietrelcina, they became tolerant of them.

Padre Pio now feared that these encounters were about to take on a new dimension.

Chapter 44

When Gena awoke that morning she had no memory of going to bed the night before. She found herself under the covers, naked. She looked around the room. *Where are my clothes? How did I get here? Oh! My head ... it hurts to move it. I must have drunk too much last night. What must he think of me? Did someone have to put me to bed? Oh, how can I face him today?* She got up and opened a dresser drawer. When she saw her clothes neatly folded away she became even more concerned. She slipped on just enough to allow her to go down the hall to the toilet that served that floor of the inn. When she came back to the room she washed and dressed herself properly.

Victoro was at the desk again when Gena came down the stairs. "Good morning. Did you sleep well?"

Gena's face reddened, "Very well. Too well I think. I can't even remember going to bed last night. I do hope I haven't anything to apologize for."

Victoro hoped that she couldn't recognize the relief he felt that she indeed couldn't remember, apparently didn't suspect…

"Believe me, you did nothing to be ashamed of. I had a wonderful evening. When you excused yourself I saw you to your door and you locked it behind you to go to bed. I hope you enjoyed yourself as much as I." *If you only knew, Gena.*

"Oh, I did. It was a wonderful evening. I just can't remember the last of it." Her face reddened a little more.

"You were awfully tired. I can understand that."

"Then no one had to help me to bed?" Gena was thinking of the clothes she found so neatly folded away.

"No. You went into your room all by yourself."

Strange, she thought, *how we do things so differently when we're unaware of our actions.* "Well, I'll try to keep better control of myself from now on," she said, smiling shyly.

"How about some breakfast?"

"I'd like that." She felt extremely hungry.

"Good, I'll join you." They went to a small table that Victoro always reserved for himself in the inn's eating area.

After breakfast Gena walked the long road back up to Saint Mary of the Graces. Again she was disappointed. Again she was assured that Padre Pio would not be able to meet with anyone for some time to come. She could not get a definite date or time when he would be available to her. No pleading of circumstance could alter the answers she got from the friars.

Disappointed, she started down the steep trail, tears in her eyes. The walk back down to San Giovanni Rotondo was as difficult as the trek up. I hate walking down hills. The footing is always so much more treacherous than going up. She was so engrossed with watching the trail that she didn't notice the robed, Capuchin friar ahead of her until she nearly ran into him.

"Gena, don't run me down."

She was startled for a moment. She could not see the face clearly, the hood hid it, but the voice was a familiar one. "Oh! I beg your pardon. I was so intent on the trail. Are you the monk I talked with yesterday? Your voice, I think I recognize it."

"No, my dear, we've not spoken in many years. I'm the friar you came here to visit."

"Padre Pio? But they told me I couldn't see you…that you'd not be out of the Cloister for a very long time. I was afraid I wouldn't get to see you at all. I'm so glad it's you, Padre Pio."

"I'm sorry about your husband's passing. He was a good man. His soul is with God."

"But how did you know? You never met him, did you? How did you know of his passing?"

"Just as I knew of your secret place in the woods so many years ago."

Gena's eyes widened. "I remember now. You described that place to me when there was no way for you to have ever seen it. Oh, Padre Pio, is his soul really with God?"

"He is with our beloved Father."

"Padre Pio, I did so want to talk with you, to make my confession to you. But they wouldn't let me. I made my confession to another Capuchin. I so wanted…"

Padre Pio interrupted, "I heard your confession to Brother Nicola, my spiritual daughter. I, too, gave you absolution."

"But how?" she didn't have to finish the question. "Thank you, Padre." She took his hand and kissed it over the fingerless mitt that he kept on to cover his wound. She was met with a beautiful fragrance from under the dressings, roses or lilacs, or their mixture.

They talked for a long time by the side of the road. All the time people were passing either going to or from the monastery. Some greeted the priest; most went by not noticing them.

"Gena, would you kneel and pray with me?" Padre Pio finally asked. "There is a roadside shrine down just' a little further."

"Yes, Padre, I would like that."

After they finished their prayer they parted. Gena started down the road. She'd only gone a few steps when she turned around to take another look at her Padre. The road was clearly visible to the wall of the monastery. Padre Pio, who could not have walked more than a few meters in the short few seconds, was nowhere to be seen.

As Gena continued down the slope and through the town to the inn, she thought of Padre Pio's caution. "Beware of the evils that lurk around you. You were once possessed by the devil, but now you will do the work of our Lord." She had asked him to explain, but he would not.

She had mentioned Victoro in their conversation and had been told, "There is much you do not know of the man. He is good within but afflicted with a curse."

"Oh, no, Padre Pio," Gena had replied in the man's defense, "he is a fine, kind man. He has treated me well, has made it possible for me to stay here longer. If it were not for him, I might not have been able to meet with you today."

"We would have met today even if you were now on the road to Pietrelcina. But if you can see the good in Victoro, that is well. I and my guardian angel will try to protect you from evil."

"But, Padre, I don't feel in any danger from Victoro." Padre Pio thought a moment, "Perhaps that is the way it is all meant to be. If you stay much longer in San Giovanni Rotondo, you will no doubt hear many stories of Victoro that will differ from your knowledge of him. Weigh all that you hear, be prudent, draw on all that you know, on all that you will learn." Again he would not elaborate.

Gena walked through the narrow streets of San Giovanni Rotondo and was excited by the activity, people going to and from, merchants buying and selling, children chasing, yelling, laughing. It was not a large town, but the biggest she had ever seen. She wanted to stay on a little longer. She was fond of Pietrelcina, but she was not ready to go back to its routine. This was the first time she'd been away from her home since she was a child and moved to the village with her parents. *How long will it be before I ever get away again? No, I'm not yet ready to go back. How I wish I could stay.* But her meager funds would not allow it.

As she approached the inn she saw Victoro crossing the road from the tavern. She felt her heart speed, pound, gladden. *How I wish I understood what Padre Pio told me.*

Victoro saw her walking and stopped midway to wait for her. He, too, had been thinking, wondering, planning how to keep her from returning to Pietrelcina. He started to walk toward her. As they neared each other, both were anxious to be together.

"Did you have a pleasant morning at the monastery?" Victoro asked, a smile on his face.

"Oh yes! I saw him. He spoke to me, prayed with me. It was a wonderful experience. He is truly a saint."

"I'm glad you got to see him, but I hope that doesn't mean you'll be going back to your village right away."

"I wish I could stay, but it's just too far beyond my means. I'm afraid I'll have to go back tomorrow. If it weren't for your kindness I'd have had to leave today. I only have enough money left to get me back to Pietrelcina."

"Well then, consider this. If you have enough to get home, then let me take care of you while you stay on here. I do want you to stay on a while. I feel we're only beginning to know each other. I enjoy your company. I want to know you better. I want you to know me better. I can well afford it. You'd be doing me a favor. I'll make you glad you stayed over."

Gena thought a moment and then agreed, "Well, all right, but just for a few days. But you must let me help you somehow. Perhaps I can work for you at the inn."

"Nonsense. You are my guest. Please, I insist." She agreed.

Chapter 45

That night clouds and a fog blew in over San Giovanni Rotondo. The moon's light was obliterated. The blackness of night had never been deeper. A chill settled over the entire area. People stayed in and shuttered their windows. Victoro and Gena ate in the inn's dining area. Up on the mountain the friars were also taking their evening meal, all but Padre Pio. He remained in his cell. He was fasting, drinking only water and the juice of a lemon. He lay on his cot, waiting, praying, listening for what he knew was inevitable tonight. His fever was rising. He'd left instructions with the Guardian Father not to allow any of the Capuchins to enter the cell, regardless of what they heard. It was an order they'd all been given many times before. They knew what it meant, but, as always, as the evening and night drew on, their anxiety grew.

This was a common experience for Padre Pio, but as frequently as it had occurred in the past, he never knew what form the demon would take, what act it would perpetrate. Usually the demons would take some grotesque, animal-like form, at times reptilian monsters would appear. Not infrequently, the demons would try to trick the priest by actually appearing as angels, saints, or some holy agents and to persuade the churchman to make some unholy pact.

Often the agent of the devil would appear as a woman to seduce the Padre.

At about 10:30 that night a putrid odor permeated the entire monastery. All the friars were aware of it. They knew what it meant. But it had never been so strong before. Most of the Capuchins gagged at the smell, some vomited. A dense green mist floated through the halls and rooms of the cloister. It was visible to all the friars. As it passed through each area, a cold chill remained in the air. Then shrieks of laughter echoed through the building. They were coming from Padre Pio's cell.

As always, the sounds were none that a human voice could make. There was crashing of furniture, cursing in a deep, guttural roar, hideous screams like those of a wild animal and occasional hissing like that of a snake. The sounds lasted only about twenty minutes this night. As always, and as promised, the Guardian Father waited at least an hour after the last sounds before he approached the closed door. He knocked and waited to hear from Padre Pio for permission to enter. This time there was no reply. He knocked again. "Padre Pio, are you alright?" There was still no answer. He waited no longer. He opened the heavy wooden door. The room was in turmoil; the Capuchin lay unconscious on the floor.

"Padre Pio, what happened to you tonight?" He ran to the priest's side. Padre Pio was on his back, his forehead bruised, and bleeding. "Do you hear me, Padre Pio? How can I help you?" He took a kerchief and pressed it to a cut on the friar's forehead. He moaned and stirred. His chair was near his head. The crucifix off the wall was still tightly clutched in his hands.

Another of the friars had come to the door now, and then a third. Together they righted his cot and laid him on it. He was coming to his senses now. "Are you all right, Padre?" One of the friars asked. "What happened? Tonight the noises were worse than usual." Padre Pio could not yet answer. When he was fully conscious a few minutes later the questions were repeated.

"The demon was irritated with me. He began to throw things about. I backed into the corner and held my crucifix between us to shield myself. That usually works, but that chair struck me a glancing blow to the head. It's the last thing I really remember."

He looked about the room at the mess, then continued, "I fear things will be more difficult for a while. He tried to sit up, but a severe pain shot through his shoulder and left arm. The Guardian Father sent one of the students for the doctor.

The friars were sitting in the dining hall when the physician came down from examining Padre Pio. "He has a dislocated shoulder and a fracture of his left clavicle," was the diagnosis.

"How do you think it happened, doctor?" The Guardian Father asked.

"Obviously, a blow broke the clavicle. Probably the chair, at the same time that it struck his head. The dislocation could have happened as he fell. It's lucky he wasn't hurt more seriously. Just what made that mess in his room? What happened up there tonight?"

No one answered. The doctor looked at each friar, waiting for an answer. He continued, "Well I guess it's one more of the mysteries surrounding the Padre. One thing is sure, though, and that is what concerns me. Those injuries could not possibly be self-inflicted, nor do I think they could have been the result of a simple accident. In my opinion, those injuries had to be caused by someone else."

The Guardian Father remained silent.

Chapter 46

After dinner, Gena again accompanied Victoro to his suite of rooms. This evening she took special care not to drink too much. Victoro was again as charming as he could be. Gena found herself falling in love with the man. Victoro sensed his victory over her emotions.

This evening he did not keep the table between them but sat down on the divan, close beside her. She was glad he did. "I'm very happy that I persuaded you to stay on," Victoro said.

"Are you sure I can't pour you a glass of wine?"

"No, thank you. I find I enjoy you more when I'm in full possession of my senses."

Victoro poured himself another glass. "I hope you don't mind if I have another."

"Not at all. Feel free to drink all you want."

"Tell me about your children, Gena."

They talked on and on into the night. At last Victoro put his arm around her shoulder and kissed her gently on the lips. She was a little surprised. She didn't protest. He kissed her again, more passionately. She felt herself wanting more. Suddenly she withdrew. "Please, Victoro, I'm sorry, I'm not ready for this. I'm afraid it's too soon. Please give me some time."

Victoro almost let his frustration show. "It's not too soon, Gena, not if you feel as I do. What I feel for you can have no time limit."

Gena didn't know how to reply to that. It sounded so logical. "Please, Victoro, let me think, please don't be angry. I feel very deeply for you, but I hardly know you. It's all happened so quickly."

Victoro decided to change his tack. "It's all right, Gena, I understand. At least have a drink with me to toast the future ... perhaps our future."

She couldn't say no to that and let him pour her a glass of the wine. In a few minutes it was relaxing her. While they talked on, he kept her glass filled. When he tried later to kiss her again she no longer resisted. But that was as far as it went that night.

When she finally excused herself to go to bed she was able to walk to her room alone. This night, Victoro had to be satisfied with voyeurism through the ventilator grate.

Chapter 47

Father Mario De Sica was gathering material hoping to prove Padre Pio a fraud, charlatan, or hysteric.

"Though all reports from physicians' examinations have indicated there was no evidence of self infliction of the wounds of the stigmata," he wrote to his superiors, "and they have not been able to show continuing irritation or chemical applications to keep the wounds open, we must still keep our minds open to those possibilities.

"More interesting are recent studies on hysteria, hypnotism and psychobiologic phenomena. It is remarkable what physical changes can be brought about in and on the human body through psychological disturbances, by mesmerism or autosuggestions, or by hysteria. Enclosed you will find case histories that illustrate each of these phenomenon. I have also included reports regarding Padre Pio of San Giovanni Rotondo.

"Careful consideration will, I believe, show that his 'miracles' can be explained by one or more of the aforementioned phenomena.

"I feel that as long as these possibilities exist, Padre Pio's restrictions should be strictly enforced. Should we be able to prove fraud in this matter, then defrocking and excommunication would be the indicated action of the Church."

The documents he enclosed were mostly from newspaper and magazine accounts, as well as letters from people who had no documentation of their claims. Documented accounts and reports were not included for his purposes.

Chapter 48.

Gena had been in San Giovanni Rotondo a little more than a week now. Victoro had still not been able to entice her into his bedchamber. It was difficult for her. She was passionate by nature and wanted him as much as he wanted her. There was no doubt in either of their minds that she loved him. And Victoro began to recognize that he was falling in love with Gena. He still lusted for her. He didn't feel any guilt about what he'd done on her first night at the inn. He felt no compunction about spying on her private moments through the ventilator grate. It didn't disturb him to use one of the tavern girls to relieve the sexual frustration he felt after Gena retired each night. The only thing that really bothered Victoro was that he was falling in love with Gena.

This night, Gena was very tired and retired early to her bed.

Victoro watched her from his secret vantage, and then headed across the road to the tavern to take his pleasure with one of the girls. As he was about to enter, Maria, one of his favorites came out the door.

"Maria, I was just coming to see you. Where are you off to so early? Let's go back in for some wine, and then some…"

"I can't tonight, Victoro. Don't be angry. My little boy is ill.

He's with my parents, and they just sent me a message to come home. Don't be angry, I have to go. You know I'd love to otherwise." There was a fearful pleading tone in her voice.

"Sure, Maria, I understand. You get right on home. If I can be of any help, let me know. When a child is sick he needs his mother at his side."

Maria was a little surprised at his understanding, relieved that he didn't create a scene. Without another word she disappeared into the darkness shrouding the road into town.

Her destination was almost to the other end of town, and she walked as rapidly as she could. It was past eleven. Almost everyone was asleep in the quiet little town. Only an occasional shuttered window let a crack of light escape. Otherwise the narrow streets of San Giovanni Rotondo were dark. All that Maria had to guide her was the light from the gas lamps that produced a dim glow at the corner of each long block she had to travel.

She hadn't gone very far from the inn when she thought she heard footsteps behind her. At first she thought nothing of it. When they turned up a side street after her it disturbed her. When they started to catch up to her she felt her pulse quicken. *Now don't let your imagination get the better of you, Maria, you've walked these streets often enough at night, and nothing's ever happened to you before.* She turned down another street along her way. When the footsteps followed her around that turn she felt the hairs on the back of her neck stand up. *Oh, God, who is that. Probably some drunk following me from the tavern. Well, I've handled drunks before, but I'm in too much of a rush tonight.* She stopped and looked back toward the light at the corner she'd just turned. He was almost upon her. She gasped in air to scream, but it was too late. He struck her a blow across the mouth that stunned her, knocked her to the ground. She was semi-conscious, felt herself being dragged into an alley, felt her clothes being torn off of her, her breasts being exposed, her panties being ripped away. She wanted to scream but, as in a nightmare, couldn't move, couldn't struggle, couldn't run.

The darkness of the alley didn't let her see her assailant. She could only feel, could only hear his panting, mumbling curses, a voice she'd never heard before, deep, hoarse, vicious. For the first time she was feeling the pain from the blow to her mouth, felt the blood, tasted it in her mouth, breathed it, and choked, coughing it out. She couldn't cry for help.

He threw himself on her. His weight was crushing her between himself and the dirt of the alley floor. Now a new terror struck at her. This fiend on top of her felt like a giant. His chest crushed down on her head while his waist, with an enormous girth, was well below her's.

Dear God, what is this thing? He slid himself up on her and she felt a fierce pressure against her genitals. It reminded her of the pressures she felt when she was giving birth, but in the wrong direction. *Oh no, he's ripping me apar …*

All her senses left her.

The first sounds to come from the alley were after sunrise. Hysterical shouting awoke most of the residents of the neighborhood, "Help, call the constable! Help, there's been a murder! Help, police! Help! Anyone, help!"

When the police arrived, a large crowd had gathered. "Please let me through! Don't anyone touch anything! Let me through."

The gathering of onlookers parted in the narrow passageway between two whitewashed stucco buildings. Their walls were splattered with blood. A larger, drying pool of gelatinous blood was on the ground, the broken body of an unclad woman in its midst.

"Get these people out of here," the chief constable commanded. The alley cleared quickly. After inspection of the scene, the body was removed to the local mortuary where a doctor examined the remains. His report shocked even the chief constable.

"The cause of death of this woman seems to have been suffocation. She partly died from drowning in her own blood, which plugged her smaller air passages, and from a crushed chest. She had a broken jaw, which was inflicted by a severe blow to her mouth before death. Three teeth were knocked out and several others loosened apparently by the same blow. A large bruise on the same side of the face showed that her blow came from an instrument larger than a fist.

"Her neck was twisted and broken, but this must have been done after death. All but three of her ribs were fractured as if she had been placed in a press, crushing her from front to back. Her liver and spleen were both ruptured by apparently the same pressure. There were no less than five fractures of her spine, also occurring some time after death. Both arms were dislocated at the shoulders as was her left hip. Her pelvis was crushed.

"The woman was a victim of rape. She had numerous tears in both her vaginal mucosa and a large tear in her anal orifice. The examining doctor could not hazard a guess at what instrument was used to cause these lesions, but there was an enormous amount of semen in both the vaginal vault and the rectum. Examination indicated that penetration of the vagina was prior to death. Anal penetration was after death.

"In my long years of experience I have never seen such a crime and cannot even hazard a guess at what monster could have perpetrated it," the report concluded.

News of the tragedy quickly spread through the town. During the investigation of Maria's last hours of life, the constable determined the time she left the tavern. The barman told of the message that came about Maria's ill son. "She left here just a little past eleven last night."

Victoro sat at a table during the inquiries. He did not volunteer the information that he'd seen her leave as he crossed the road, that he'd spoken with her, that he'd wanted her last night.

Chapter 49

Panic swept the town when a second and third body was found in a field just outside San Giovanni Rotondo that afternoon. She was a woman of about twenty-seven or eight. She'd been going back to her village after her pilgrimage to the monastery. Her nine-year-old son had accompanied her. His body was found nearby, killed by a single blow to the head.

The doctor's examination led to a similar report as that of Maria's death. "There is no doubt that the same fiend killed these two. Both the mother and child died this morning, several hours after the first murder," he told the constable as he handed him his formal, handwritten report. "She, too, had a torn vaginal vault and anus."

"Could it be just from the forcible entry?" the constable asked.

Rape certainly can cause tears and tissue damage," the doctor affirmed, "but these tears are far greater than any I've ever seen due to penetration. Tears like that would require a penis the size of a horse's. No, I can't believe the rape alone could have caused them."

"How big would a man have to be?"

"What do you mean?"

"How big, to have an organ that large?"

"Are you serious? It's impossible."

"Maybe so, but how big would such a man have to be?"

The doctor looked at the constable. "All right, I'll play your little game," and he thought a few moments, "if I consider the smallest penis that could cause such damage, he would still have to be a giant, eight feet tall at the very least."

"How much would such a monster weigh?"

"What are you driving at?"

"How much would he weigh?" the constable repeated.

"Hell, I don't know, maybe three-fifty, four hundred pounds, maybe more if he were well-muscled."

"Why well-muscled?"

"Muscle weighs more than fat."

"How much then if he were well-muscled?"

"Could be five to six hundred pounds, I guess. Why?"

"Would that much weight crush a woman if she were on a hard surface?"

"Easily. Jesus, you don't honestly think we're dealing with a monster like that, do you?"

The constable didn't answer, just shrugged his shoulders as he thought about what the doctor said.

At about eight o'clock that evening, shrieks of terror shattered the silent town. They echoed up and down the narrow streets. No one could tell just where they came from. Three or four of them, then silence again. That cleared the streets of the few people who were still out. Shutters closed everywhere. Only the constable and the two policemen who were on duty went in search. After half an hour they returned to the station house.

They didn't even know in which direction to look. They'd knocked on doors and asked those inside from which direction the screams had come. The answers were from every point of the compass.

In the morning the third body was discovered, again in an alley. The medical report was almost a duplicate of the others.

"You are not to go out on the streets alone, Gena," Victoro demanded, "not during the night or day. Not until they catch this maniac."

"I assure you I won't. It's awful what he's done to those women, to that child, to this town. I promise I'll not set foot outside unless you're with me!"

Victoro felt better. He found his concern for Gena's welfare out of character. How long had it been since he'd given a second thought to anyone else? What was it that was so different about her? The longer she held off his advances, the more he wanted her, the more he cared for her. But the worst part was that other women no longer excited him. While making love to his "regular" ladies, he found his thoughts drifting to Gena.

A sinister sensation swept through his soul, turning his thoughts of compassion into those of extreme resentment. He would tolerate no more. Does she think her body is some sort of a prize? I am tired of playing the game. This night he would fulfill his passions.

Chapter 50

"Padre Pio, you've never visited me before ... I have never even seen you down here in San Giovanni. To what can I credit this great honor?"

The chief constable was alone in his office. He knew the Capuchin well, and was overwhelmed by the visit.

"I am here about the trouble, the murders."

"You have some information about the murders?"

"Look to a giant in a neighboring village," Pio suggested. "He is a tormented, bitter man. He will go with you peaceably when confronted. Do not use excessive force. Prejudice and ridicule have made him what he is."

"But how do you know all this? What village?"

"Where the fair is!"

"A fair? Where is there a fair?"

Padre Pio said no more, but turned and went out of the office door. By the time the chief constable got up, rounded his desk, and crossed his office, the station house was empty.

"Which way did he go?" the constable called to an officer loitering in a corner with a magazine.

"Which way did who go, sir?" a surprised, confused policeman asked. "Padre Pio, who else has come through here in the last hour?"

"Padre Pio? I've not seen Padre Pio. No one's been in here all afternoon. I've been sitting here. I've seen no one."

"Stupid! He just came through here from my office." And with that the constable ran out into the street. He looked both ways. The street was empty. "That's impossible. He couldn't have gotten out of sight that quickly, not with his limping, shuffling gait. It's impossible."

There was indeed a fair in a neighboring village. It had been there for more than a week, a traveling fair. Among its wonders was a giant. A man afflicted with pituitary hormone disease.

"Acromegaly," the doctor called it after the man had been arrested. "He's what is known medically as a pituitary giant. A rare disease caused by a tumor of the pituitary gland which produces an excess of growth hormone."

The arrest went just as Padre Pio had predicted. When the giant was confronted, he broke down and cried, said he was glad it was over, welcomed being caught. Afterward, the chief constable went up the mountain to see Padre Pio to report the arrest and thank him for his help. He also wanted to ask Pio how he knew. He was left speechless when told that Padre Pio could not be seen and that he had not been out of the chapel for the entire afternoon in which he was supposed to have been in San Giovanni Rotondo.

Chapter 51

The evening began like so many others, with wine, talk, laughter, and occasional kisses. But this evening was to be different. Shortly after dinner, Gena accompanied Victoro to his suite for what he termed "A little more wine and conversation." She did not see him lock the door behind them.

As she sat down on the small couch situated at the far side of the room, she turned to see that he was still by the door. He'd slipped his shoes off, and was now unbuttoning his shirt.

Gena was horrified. The warm, understanding face she'd admired across the table at dinner was now replaced with one, which was cold and cruel. "Victoro!" she gasped, "what do you think you are doing?"

Victoro's expression did not change as he loosened his belt and removed his pants. Gena stood to her feet and made a beeline towards the door. "I am going now, Victoro."

"Not until I get what I want, what I deserve!" he bellowed. Gena grasped the doorknob, but it would not turn. "Let me out, please!"

Victoro let out a small, cool chuckle. "Wouldn't you like a little dessert before you leave, Gena?" He was holding his erection in his hand. Victoro grabbed Gena's arm and dragged her over to his bed, whereupon he swung her atop the quilted spread.

"Victoro! For the love of God, leave me be!" she cried.

"For the love of God? Why not for the love of me! You want it just as bad as I, Gena. You're going to get it, so why not enjoy it?" Victoro lurched onto the bed and began tearing Gena's blouse off. She resisted with all her might, trying to roll to her stomach, but she was no match for his strength. Sliding his right hand under her dress until it stopped, he proceeded to direct two fingers around her panties and into her warm envelope.

Gena stopped struggling. Her breathing became very heavy as Victoro's fingers explored every crevice. The hot moisture, which flowed from within heightened Victoro's excitement, and he began ripping the remainder of her clothing from her body.

Gena laid still. *Padre Pio warned me. Why didn't I listen? But he never said this would happen. Oh Padre! You knew all along. But where are you now, when I need you?*

"Victoro!" Victoro jerked his head around to see a man hooded and cloaked in the brown robes of a Capuchin. He froze. Gena slid slowly off the bed, clutching what little clothes remained close to her half-clad body.

"You have been singing hymns to the Devil, Victoro!" The figure came forward from the shadow. It was Padre Pio. "Leave me alone, please. I'll let her be, I promise! Just leave me alone!" Victoro hid his face with his hands and began backing up to the headboard. He grabbed a quilt and covered himself with it. "Please, Padre. P-Please leave me alone."

Gena stood with her back to the wall, watching with disbelief as the man so violent a moment ago cowered himself before the priest. Pio lifted the quilt and threw it to the floor.

"Leave us alone! Leave us alone!" Victoro's mouth was moving, but it wasn't his voice. In fact, many voices were coming from his throat, all at the same time, like a spoken chorus.

Pio ignored the voices. He began making the sign of the cross over Victoro while at the same time saying prayers in Latin.

Gena stood transfixed as Victoro let out a fierce cry of pain. The large picture window shattered, as if a force within the room was making a terrified exit.

Then it was over. Victoro rolled from the bed and on to the floor before Pio's feet.

"Forgive me, Padre." He began whimpering, and then sobbing. "I am sorry. So, so, sorry!"

Pio directed his attention to Gena. "Please go to your room, child. I must hear our friend's confession. I have waited so long."

The newspapers picked up the story of Padre Pio's part in the arrest of the giant. Though he made no statement, the press made it look as though Pio had given "exclusive interviews."

When Father Mario De Sica read the accounts he became furious. "This fraud of a priest is after nothing but his own glorification. He must be stopped. Excommunication is too good for him!"

Part III

Chapter 52

Victoro and Gena's wedding was saddened only by the fact that Padre Pio could neither perform the marriage nor be present at the holy celebration. Shortly after the wedding, Gena's children came to live with them in San Giovanni Rotondo. Victoro sold the tavern but kept the inn to which he made an addition. He never told Gena of the ventilator, but had it sealed off. The day after his exorcism, he went to his mother and begged her forgiveness. He tried the best he could to make amends around the town. Some people seemed to forgive easily; some would have nothing to do with him. He couldn't give a logical explanation for his years of sin and strange behavior. Only time and years of exemplary conduct might change their minds.

After Padre Pio's intervention with Victoro, his battles with the demons became more violent, but his greatest problem seemed to come from the Holy Office of the Vatican.

There were constant appeals from the public to the Church to free Padre Pio from his restrictions. Appeals also went to the government. The letters came by the thousands. Finally the government took an interest, and

Mussolini's office made an official appeal to the Pope. Pope Pius XI could no longer ignore the matter. He demanded a complete review of Padre Pio's life and activities. Preparation of that report would take almost two years, and Father Mario De Sica's contribution would only be a part.

Chapter 53

Monsignor Damino had followed Pio's life very closely. He had first met the Padre in 1919, less than a year since the stigmata had appeared, and had the pleasure of speaking with him for over two hours. The two men seemed to hit it off immediately, and within the two hours they had developed a close friendship. Over the years, Damino and Pio exchanged letters until the Church ordered Pio's contact with the outside world to cease.

One day, after reading a newspaper account disclaiming Padre Pio, Damino became deeply saddened. He missed the letters. He knew in his heart that Pio was a special gift from God to the people. Depressed, the Monsignor walked the garden of the Vatican. The tranquil surroundings of the garden relaxed him. He sat down to rest on an ornate stone bench located near the center of the garden. The flowers smell so fragrant today! Never before have they sent such sweetness into my nostrils. As he stared at the ground, he observed the shadow of someone standing behind him.

He turned. "Padre Pio!"

"Do you think our friendship stopped simply because the letters had to stop? The monk asked.

"Please ... sit with me, Padre!" The monsignor slid over on the bench, making room for his friend. He turned to repeat the invitation, but Pio had disappeared.

The garden was very large; there was no possible way that Padre Pio could have walked out of his sight within that split moment. The Monsignor smiled. His friend hadn't forgotten him.

Monsignor Damino visited the monastery of Our Lady of Grace again in 1931. When he saw Pio, he immediately questioned him about the visit in the garden. "Padre, I know you have not been outside these walls. Yet I saw you and heard you speak. I did see you, didn't I?"

"But it is as you say, Monsignor ... I have not left this place."

"Then you are saying that I did not receive a visit from you?" Pio laughed. "What you are trying to ask me now is 'Am I going mad?' No, my friend, you are not."

Monsignor Damino had no reservations about relating his supernatural experience with Pio to his fellow clergymen. The Pontiff, not completely immune from the stories, which spread within the walls of the papal city, heard of the encounter and summoned the Monsignor to his office.

"It has been rumored that you have seen and spoke to Padre Pio of Pietrelcina right here in the Holy City."

"Yes, Your Holiness."

"If you say it is so, I believe it." The Pope rubbed his hands together thoughtfully before he continued to speak.

"Monsignor," he began in a soft voice, as if what he were about to say was to be held in strict confidence, "did you ever know **Monsignor Lavitrano of Bari**?"

"I met him only once, and that was about seven years ago. I understand he passed away last spring."

"Yes. Did you know he visited Padre Pio frequently?"

"No, Your Holiness."

"I'm sorry, how could you. He had a great respect for the padre; a respect that some do not share. He was getting on in years, and he told Padre Pio that when he retired it would be in San Giovanni Rotondo, so that Pio could assist him at his death. But the Padre told Monsignor Lavitrano it was not possible, for the Monsignor would die in Uruguay. But Pio promised he would assist him there. As you probably know, it was in Uruguay that he did die, at a ceremony dedicating a new seminary."

Monsignor Damino nodded his head but said nothing, anxious to hear the Pontiff continue his story.

"On the night of his death, a young priest, who was lodging in the same Episcopal residence, was awakened by someone knocking at his door. It was a Capuchin monk, later identified as Padre Pio telling him that the Monsignor was dying. The young priest quickly awakened some of the other clergymen in the building and rushed to the Monsignor's room. But the Monsignor had already passed on."

Monsignor Damino had absorbed every word, and was elated in the fact that this incident would give credence to his own personal encounter with Pio.

"Did anyone else besides the young priest see the padre, Your Holiness?"

The Pontiff leaned forward and opened the top drawer of his massive, heavily ornamented desk and brought forth a small piece of paper, which he handed the Monsignor. "This was removed from Monsignor Lavitrano's personal note pad. The handwriting has been verified as his own. It was found clutched in his fist when they discovered his body."

Monsignor Damino gazed hypnotically at the scribbled words, "Padre Pio came."

The Pontiff stood and extended his hand for the return of the note. "This seems to be an incredible man, Monsignor. Are you aware he has the gift of tongues?"

The Monsignor passed the note back. "No, Your Holiness ... I was not aware..."

"The Superior at the monastery confirmed the rumor in a letter to me. Our Padre can speak and understand any language fluently, although he has never studied any language other than Italian and Latin."

"Just as the..."

The Pontiff read the Monsignor's thoughts. "Yes. Just as the Apostles."

In the spring of 1933, Pope Pius XI read his decision. Father Mario was among those present when it was delivered. The Pontiff looked directly at Father Mario and spoke, **"Ho non sono stato maldisposito del Padre Pio, ma io sono stato malin formato del Padre Pio. (I have not been badly disposed to Padre Pio, but I have been badly informed of Padre Pio.")**

Padre Pio's long confinement was over. He received permission to celebrate Mass and twelve months later he received permission to hear confessions from men. A few months passed before being allowed to hear confessions from women. Shortly thereafter, all of his priestly privileges were returned to him. When it became common knowledge that the Capuchin was back on his pulpit and returned to the confessional booth, throngs of pilgrims kept a constant procession to the church of Saint Mary of the Graces and to the little town of San Giovanni Rotondo.

Chapter 54

Father Mario could not get over the slap he felt with the Pope's declaration. He was not ready to give up. Now he was more determined than ever to prove the friar-priest a fraud.

In 1935 he arranged to make a trip to San Giovanni Rotondo and see the Capuchin himself. There would be no advance warning that he was coming. He'd observe the friar in secret, and when he was ready he would reveal himself and get answers to questions that had been bothering him for years. So determined was he to keep the trip a secret that he didn't even tell his superiors where he was going. "Just a long-needed vacation," he told everyone.

"Where to? Oh, no place in particular. I just plan to travel around the country, maybe visit with some old friends and see some of the people I've corresponded with through the years."

Father Mario boarded a train in Rome and took it to Foggia. From there he would have to take a bus or taxi to San Giovanni Rotondo. He'd take a room at an inn and obtain information from the townspeople about the Padre. Of course he would have to dress other than as a priest until he revealed his true identity. Only then would he again put on his priestly garb.

The train arrived at Foggia late in the evening, just before ten. As Father Mario disembarked, a chubby, red-faced man with a big grin on his face approached. "Father Mario, Father Mario, over here. I have a car for you. Let me take your baggage."

The priest was stunned. *How could this stranger know me, be expecting me, and be waiting for me with a car?*

"I beg your pardon, but how do you know me?" the overwhelmed priest asked.

"You're just as Padre Pio described. Dressed exactly as he said you'd be. He even told me which rail car you'd be on. No way I could have missed you, Father."

"But that's impossible, I told no one…"

"Well, all I know, Father, is that Padre Pio told me where to be and how to find you. And here I am, and here you are. Now let me take your bag, and follow me to the car."

Father Mario was too shocked to refuse. He handed the jolly man his bag and followed. *If this Capuchin knows that I was on the train and how I would be dressed, then he knows why I'm here. No doubt the priest has the power of e.s.p.; a true gift, yes; but not necessarily a gift from heaven.* Father Mario was disturbed. Realizing that he was beginning to doubt the convictions, which he had held so tightly over the years made him very uncomfortable. I will not fall for these tricks. I am right!

He drove to Victoro's inn and there let Father Mario off. "It's too late to climb the road to the friary tonight, Father. Padre Pio has arranged a room and meal for you here. Early tomorrow, Victoro, the owner, or his wife, Gena, will accompany you to the monastery where Padre Pio looks forward to your visit."

His identity no longer a secret, Father Mario donned his priestly garb the next morning. He was awakened early to be in time for Padre Pio's Mass. Both Victoro and Gena decided to attend, so both accompanied him to the monastery. They also brought a helper from the inn to carry the priest's baggage. It was arranged that Mario would spend the rest of his nights at the friary.

The Mass was the most inspiring Father Mario had ever attended. As it was drawing to a conclusion, his anxiety grew. Never had he seen anyone serve Mass with more heartfelt emotion. Even Father Mario's own ordination had not moved him so. Padre Pio's love for God was evident in his every word, in his every expression and movement. Tears of love, anguish, joy, and pain flowed freely from the friar's eyes, his heart.

Chapter 55

Pio turned and faced the people to give the last blessing. As he was making the sign of the cross, an outburst of heavy sobbing emanated from a man situated in the third pew. It was Father Mario.

Every eye in the small church, filled with curiosity, watched as the distraught Mario exited through the side door, which led to the garden. Brother Nicola followed, and once outside found Father Mario sitting on a small wooden bench under the large cypress tree located in the center of the small garden. Father Mario was still weeping, holding his face in his hands as he stared down at the ground.

Brother Nicola laid his hand on the man's shoulders. "What troubles you, Father? Are you not well?"

Father Mario looked up to see who was speaking. Recognizing the man as one of the Capuchin brothers, he clutched Nicola's arm with both hands, his tearful eyes begging for answers. "Did you see? Didn't everybody see Pio as I did? Please I beg you tell me!"

"What is it you speak of Father? I do not understand…"

"Then you didn't see it! At the last blessing ... Padre Pio ... His head was covered with ... with ... a crown of thorns! Blood was running down, all over his face! When he outstretched his arms, I saw him nailed to a large cross! Why didn't anybody else see? I have been cursed! I…" Father Mario buried his face in his hands and began weeping even harder. As he thought back on how he had slandered the priest, his anguish deepened.

It was several minutes later when Father Mario began to regain his composure. He stood and wiped his eyes and wet face with his handkerchief. He was alone. Brother Nicola had left. He began pacing the garden. He was too absorbed with his guilt to appreciate the well-kept flowers. He couldn't hear the chirp of the birds for the reproach he heaped on himself. What was he to do now? I must leave this place at once. Suddenly he was aware of an aroma he'd never before experienced. He turned to see its source and saw only Padre Pio.

The friar limped toward Father Mario with outstretched arms.

Chapter 56

"My dear Father Mario," he said, as if to an old friend, "I am happy to finally meet you." He embraced his guest, and the guest felt a warmth, a security, a love, as a child feels with his father. His anxiety melted away.

"Padre, I have so much to apologize to you for. Where can I begin?"

"Nonsense. You did what you had to do. It was your job."

"But Padre, I did it with malice. I did it from envy. I sinned. I did bear false witness against you. And today, with my own eyes, saw you upon a cross with a crown of thorns. I fear I have been cursed!"

"You have not been cursed, Father, but rather blessed. Today God gave you a small miracle. Thank Him for it."

Tears began to form again in Father Mario's eyes. "Padre, how can you accept me now, after what I have done?"

A small smile crossed Pio's lips. "We are all brothers in the eyes of God, and I cannot but love my brother. My restrictions were the will of God. They had their purpose. You were but an instrument of our Father. But that is behind us now."

There was a short silence and the two men embraced once more. Then Padre Pio spoke again, "I must go to the confessional booth. You see the lines of people who do me the honor."

"And I wish you do me the honor of hearing my confession, Padre."

"Gladly, my brother; this evening we will have time to speak, to pray together. But now I will take you to Brother Nicola who will settle you in and show you about. He will make you at home while I earn my keep."

Father Mario was taken to his cell, then given a tour of the monastery. Then he and Brother Nicola went outside of the high walls of the compound. They walked by the church, Saint Mary of the Graces. Lines of people snaked from the mountain road to the church entrance.

"So many people," Father Mario observed.

"Thousands each day. They come from everywhere. Some are only curious. Some come for the Mass, some just to pray in the church and many to confess through Padre Pio."

"How many can he confess?"

"About 70 a day…and they come back day after day until they can have their turn…rich, poor, it matters not. To him they are each his spiritual children, and most go away with renewed faith, a rekindled spirit."

Father Mario thought for a moment. 'Yes, I understand their feeling."

"Come, let us go up the mountain. From there we can see clear to the sea if the day is right."

They walked up the narrow path. The mountain was bare of trees, denuded over the centuries by the people of the area in need of wood for fuel and building. There was a constant breeze off the **Gulf of Manfredonia**, even though it was more than twenty-five kilometers to the east.

"Tell me about Padre Pio. I mean about the things that aren't in the papers, things you know first-hand. You've known him a long while, I assume."

"Since he first came here. I was the one who found him the day he was stigmatized. Things here ... our lives ... everything has changed so much since then."

"Is it really true, the struggles he has at night with the demons. Is it really as rumored?"

"Nothing you could read would describe that adequately. Sounds out of a horror story emanate from that cell, incredible, inhuman sounds. We can accept them, but not get used to them. They are a part of our lives here. Maybe you'll see. It occurs several times a month."

"But if it is so violent, why isn't he hurt?"

"Often he is injured, bruised, or cut. Once he had a dislocation and fracture. He is able to ward the demons off with his faith. He frustrates them. That is when the noise and profanities start. They start out to tempt him, seduce him, then intimidate him. When they fail, the violence begins."

"But why?"

"Perhaps it is to test him ... to test his faith, his loyalty. Who knows? These are not earthly matters, not for us to understand."

"And what of the miracles, the cures, do you know of them first hand?"

"Many, many. They are a weekly occurrence. We witness them all the time."

"Real cures? Not just hysterical, imaginary illnesses, feigned disease?"

"Let me tell you of a typical case ... it involved both

Cardinal

D'Indico of Florence, and **bilocation**. It was July 20th, 1921."

"I know of Cardinal D'Indico, but I know of no illness he had," Father Mario interjected.

"It was his sister. She was on her deathbed on that date. The Cardinal sat in his study waiting for the priest to come down from his sister's room. She'd been given up by the doctors and had been given her last rights. She was terminal with tuberculosis, and already in a deep coma. From his study he could see the door to her room. He'd been in her room all evening, but his sorrow was too great so the Cardinal decided to leave for a while. He told the young priest who was keeping the vigil with him to call immediately if there was a change in her condition.'

"He was dumbfounded when the door to her room opened and a friar in Capuchin robe stepped out. He watched him walk down the stairs and past the open study door. When he looked in, the Cardinal recognized him as Padre Pio.

"'Cardinal', the friar said, 'Go to her, her coma is over. Her fever is broken. In a few days she will be cured of her disease.'

"The man thought he was surely hallucinating, especially when the friar walked on and was out of sight by the time the Cardinal got into the hallway. Nevertheless, he ran to her room."

"As he burst through the door he saw the woman was fully awake. 'I have seen Padre Pio' she said. 'He came to me while I was asleep. He told me I would be well. He took my confession and gave me his blessing.'

"Cardinal D'Indico turned to the priest, 'Have you seen Padre Pio?'

"I've seen no one. I admit I dozed, but had anyone been here, I'm sure I'd have known. I awoke as soon as she came out of her coma.'

"Just as Padre Pio predicted, the woman was diagnosed as completely cured within the week. Even her doctors admitted that only a miracle could have saved her life, much less cure her completely."

Father Mario listened quietly to the story. Brother Nicola could see a deep sense of atonement in his eyes. With an understanding smile, he said "Father Mario, such miracles occur often here at Saint Mary of the Graces. I have seen with my own eyes. Granted, some are surely hysterics, but many more are real. They are people on whom doctors have given up. This is their last hope. They get well with Pio's blessing. At times he looks at a person and tells them what treatment they need. They go back and tell their doctors, and the cures are successful. We have documentation of such incidents from some of the finest specialists in the country."

The sun sent warm rays down on the two, but the breeze from the gulf cooled them. Brother Nicola shielded his eyes and looked up at several sea gulls circling overhead. "It always amazes me how far inland they fly. They are such graceful birds."

Father Mario changed the subject. "Does he suffer from his wounds?"

"I understand the pain is excruciating. He will not talk about it, but I know he bears pain no other mortal could tolerate."

"Why do you say that?"

"In 1925 Padre Pio had a hernia that strangulated. He was having severe pains, and we called **Dr. Giorgio**

Festa to examine him. The physician said that he would have to have an emergency operation immediately to avoid gangrene of the bowel. 'We must get him to a hospital right away. I must operate within the hour.'

"That was when Padre was under the most severe restriction. He refused to leave the monastery. 'I am under obedience. You will have to operate here.'

"The doctor agreed that he could get his instruments up here to do the surgery but that he could not get the anesthetic from the hospital in time.

"'Then you will have to do it without anesthetic,' Padre Pio insisted. The doctor wanted to refuse, but the Padre is a stubborn man. 'It is the will of God. It is the only way I will allow it.' We all tried to persuade him otherwise, but soon it became evident that this was the only way.

While Dr. Festa went for his equipment we set up a makeshift operating room after the doctor's instructions. The doctor said that he would start the operation only if Padre Pio agreed to go to the hospital immediately if the pain was more than he could bear. The bargain was struck."

"When we were out of the room the doctor told me to make arrangements to move Pio to the hospital, that he would be ready to go as soon as the first incision was made.

"Well, the operation started. Tears filled the Padre's eyes, but he didn't whimper, didn't move. The doctor hesitated after the first incision. 'Padre, please, the pain must be excruciating. Please reconsider.' Padre Pio only said, 'Dr. Festa, please do not drag this suffering out. God's will be done.' After that, the surgeon worked as fast as he could to complete the operation. Tears remained in Pio's eyes throughout the surgery, but he uttered only an occasional moan. He suffered the painful surgery for over two hours. After it was over, he joked with the doctor, 'Now doctor, it is your turn for the surgery to have your own hernia repaired.'

"Dr. Festa insisted that he'd never discussed his hernia with Padre Pio, but that he did indeed have one."

"I am curious, Brother Nicola, did his surgery heal normally?"

Brother Nicola laughed, "That is the first question anyone asks who hears that Pio had surgery. Even Dr. Festa wondered whether there would be a problem healing afterwards, or whether the incision would stay open like the stigmata. Actually, it healed perfectly, and faster than normal."

Chapter 57

The years after Padre Pio's restrictions were lifted were relatively good ones for the Capuchin, perhaps the best. He was able to work among his people. His adversaries were somewhat quieted. He had reasonable control over the demons. But that lasted only a short time. On October 3, 1935, Italy went back to war. Padre Pio's respite was over. Benito Mussolini invaded Ethiopia.

Though the Capuchins disassociated themselves from politics, Padre Pio could not ignore a madness that was going to cost the lives of tens of thousands of young Italians. He was vocal about the stupidity of the invasion. He told one of the other friars, "I know that Mussolini was instrumental in getting the Pope to reopen my case and eventually lift my restrictions. That was one of the smart things he did. On the other hand, this invasion of Ethiopia was one of the more stupid moves on his part."

"War is always stupid," the other friar said.

"Yes, but this will have much farther reaching repercussions than settling a border conflict with Italian Somaliland. It is a prelude to a greater war to come. The most horrible war the world has ever seen is on the horizon, and because of what has happened today, we will be allied with the wrong side."

"A greater war? What war?"

"We are on the brink of another world conflict, a World War

II. Millions will die in battle, millions will die of starvation, millions will die in the path of the conflict, and a madman will butcher more millions for their political and religious beliefs. That madman will be Mussolini's only support in this slaughter he has perpetrated today. What he has yet to learn is that his one supporter is to be a friend of little loyalty."

Of course, the other friar had no idea that the madman Padre Pio referred to was **Adolf Hitler.**

Padre Pio explained to the other friars that it was not just a simple border skirmish but a war brought on by Mussolini's own ego. "He cannot forget that in 1889 **Ethiopia's King Menelik II** defeated the Italian border army in Somaliland with a crushing offensive, when they repeatedly encroached on Ethiopian territory. Now there has been renewed tension on that border, and Mussolini takes advantage of it to avenge that old humiliation. He does not realize the far-reaching effect this terrible act of vengeance will have."

The initial attack penetrated deep into Ethiopia. Italian mechanized forces, supported by air strikes and backed by infantry, overwhelmed the primitive, ill-trained army of Ethiopia. Ethiopia fought with outmoded weapons, many the same as those used in their victory in the late nineteenth century. The Italians overwhelmed and struck deep, but they did not defeat. Their offensive bogged down, and the Ethiopians had a chance to regroup, resupply and appeal to the League of Nations. That appeal did little other than bring economic sanctions against Italy, which were hardly enforced, and threats from Great Britain and reprimands from the United States and a few other of the member nations.

Hitler sat on the sidelines watching very closely. He was letting his ally test the water. The reaction of the rest of the world to this outrageous attack on Ethiopia would give him the courage to carry out his own future expansionistic plans.

Hitler was especially interested in Great Britain's threats. He openly supported Italy with encouragement and raw materials. In secret, he supplied Ethiopia with arms and supplies to keep the war going, at least long enough to see whether the British would carry out their threats. When they didn't, he knew that he'd be able to negotiate with England while he invaded other European countries. They would not enter a war until he was ready for them.

Padre Pio had foreseen this one-sided alliance. When World War II broke out in 1939, Hitler reminded Mussolini that he had supported him in 1935. The die had been cast. Italy was allied with Germany against most of the world.

Italy also was torn internally between fascism and communism. It was a time when the wealthy exerted tremendous political power, when the poor were terribly oppressed, and the middle class were quickly joining the ranks of the poverty-stricken. It was a perfect medium for communism to take root. The nation was polarizing the few fabulously wealthy and the government against the millions of poor living under economic and political oppression.

It was an embarrassing position for the Church. As horrible as she found fascism to be, coexistence between the Church and communism was impossible. Her policy of staying out of politics was now more than ever enforced. Because of his oath of obedience to the Church, Padre Pio, along with the other churchmen, kept many of those thoughts to himself. His conscience left him all at ease. He especially disliked the pact the Vatican had made with Hitler, the **Concordats of 1933.**

"On July 20 of 1933," Padre Pio announced to his Brothers, "Pope Pius XI has signed a Concordat with the madman of Germany, Adolf Hitler, that will bind us to silence when we will want to cry out. We will witness in the coming years the worst crimes against humanity the world has ever known, and we will have to keep to ourselves the condemnation of those atrocities."

"What pact?" Brother Nicola asked. "What is in the pact that silences us?"

"Simply put, the pact agrees to keep the Church and its priests out of Hitler's politics, and in return Hitler will not interfere with the policies of the Vatican and the **Roman Catholic Church**."

"How did they ever get Pope Pius XI to agree to such a pact?"

"Actually, it was negotiated by **Cardinal Pacelli**," Padre Pio explained. "Before he became Cardinal in 1929, he was *Archbishop of Sardes* and *Apostolic Nuncio to Germany*. In 1925 he moved to Berlin. A year after he became Cardinal, he became **Secretary of State to the Vatican**. In that capacity he negotiated the Concordat between the Holy See and the Third Reich. It was signed by him and **Hitler's Vice Chancellor von Papen** on June 20th, 1930."

"But the pact was not signed by the Pope," one of the friars commented. "Couldn't the Pope rescind what he has not himself signed?"

Padre Pio became quiet, as if he hadn't even heard the question, as if he were unaware of the others in the room, as if his mind were elsewhere. Then he looked at the friar and said, "It doesn't work that way, but it wouldn't matter. Pope Pius XI will not live long enough to see the horror, and in 1939 Cardinal Pacelli will become **His Holiness, Pope Pius XII**."

A hush fell over the room at the prophecy.

In 1939 Pope Pius XI died. Cardinal Pacelli became Pope Pius XII. The pact stood.

Chapter 58

After her experience with Ethiopia, Italy decided to remain neutral at the outset of World War II. But by June 10, 1940, she had been drawn in by Germany and declared war against both France and Great Britain. By September 27 of that same year she had been included in a three-power pact with Germany and Japan, making her a full partner in Hitler's war. On June 22, 1941, she declared war on Russia. The United States of America was not to be spared, and on December 11, 1941, she joined her ally Japan and declared war on the Americans.

But World War II was Mussolini's game. The people of Italy had little stomach for the war. Fascism had not been that popular with the majority of the people before the war, and Nazism was very alien to them. When the tide of the conflict went against Germany in 1943 and Sicily was invaded on July 1Oth, internal political turmoil took place in Italy. **King Victor Emmanuel** and the **Fascist Grand Council** forced Mussolini's resignation. The new government dissolved the Fascist party and put Mussolini under arrest. On September 3, 1943, Southern Italy was invaded, and five days later the new government surrendered the country.

September 8th was the date of the surrender, but not the end of the war for the people of Italy. It was only the beginning of their hardship. Germany had not been a particularly friendly ally; now she became a horrible enemy. The Germans rescued Mussolini, made him head of a new government of Northern Italy, and quickly occupied all of Italy to several kilometers south of Rome.

Now the Americans and British were bombing and shelling the North of Italy, and the Germans were bombing and shelling the entire South, and they destroyed everything that they left behind as they retreated. As Padre Pio had predicted years earlier, of those who were not killed in battle or by bombings and shelling, so many died of starvation and illness.

Chapter 59

Michael Devino had been amongst the crowd for more than an hour, trying desperately to inch his way towards the monk. But it was futile, for it seemed like everyone else was trying to do the same. His frustration mounted when Pio departed the garden and entered the confessional booth. Now it would be hours before the monk would surface again, and the prospect of seeing Pio seemed almost nonexistent. Could he have forgotten?

Exactly one year earlier, Michael and his wife, **Andrina,** did have the fortunate pleasure of meeting the Padre in the same garden. It was only a brief encounter, but it would be carved deeply in their hearts for the rest of their lives. Immediately after Pio's Mass had ended that morning, the couple hastily made their way to the door from which Pio would exit. A few moments later, a small crowd had gathered beside them with the same intention of seeing, and perhaps exchanging words with the stigmatized priest. When the Padre did appear, the crowd jumped forward and surrounded him. Michael and Andrina found themselves being pushed further and further away from Pio as the crowd grew in size. The young couple stood back in disappointment. They had heard about Pio's gift of prophecy, and were hoping for the opportunity to speak to him about children. After six years of marriage, they were still without.

"Michael," came a voice from the center of the crowd. "Michael and Andrina, come over here!" The voice belonged to Padre Pio.

The couple looked at each other questionably. Surely the priest was not referring to them; they had never met before. But as the nucleus of the crowd began coming towards them, their hearts pounded with optimism.

"Do you not know your own names?" Padre Pio stepped forward and smiled at Michael and Andrina. They stood speechless. The priest chuckled. "Bring him to me one year from today and I will baptize him." With these words, the padre turned and moved away with the crowd.

The year had passed. Ten days earlier, Andrina had given birth to a boy, whom the couple named Pio. Michael's head hung low as he entered the sacristy where his wife had been waiting with the infant.

"Michael, where have you been?" There was a hint of annoyance in her voice.

He was surprised at the tone she was taking. "I've been trying to get to Padre Pio, but, with the crowd, it seems as though it is going to be impossible."

"Impossible? What are you talking about? Padre Pio was here thirty minutes ago. You missed the baptismal ceremony!" Michael Devino was stupefied. He did not doubt the words of his wife, nor the words of his brother who was present as the infant's godfather. But for the last hour, his eyes had been glued to the padre. Pio had never left the garden during the time his wife had claimed the baby was baptized.

Chapter 60

The war created a conflict for Padre Pio, between obedience and humanity. In 1938, nearly 60,000 Jews lived in Italy. They represented only one-tenth of one percent of the entire nation's population. Most lived in the large cities such as Rome, Milan, Trieste, Florence. They had been accepted into the society and economy of Italy for centuries. Unlike most of Europe, Italy was not a particularly anti-Semitic country. By the time she entered the war, more than 10,000 Jews from other European countries had sought and found refuge in Italy. When Italy became allied with Germany, she was forced to change her policies.

A number of antiJewish laws were passed. Jews were excluded from civil service, military service, political party membership, were not allowed to own establishments or businesses employing more than just a very few Italian non-Jews. Professionals could not practice except on other Jews, marriages between Jews and non-Jews were forbidden, and strict limitations were placed on property owned by Jews. It was a devastating blow that plunged most Jewish people into poverty and unbearable hardship. Because of the concordats, the Church remained silent.

The people of Italy also had to keep quiet, but at least many of them acted. When Hitler's Gestapo and SS ordered the Jews deported to concentration camps and work camps, and finally death camps, many Italians did what they could to hide Jews and gave them refuge.

Victoro and Gena came to Padre Pio one day early in 1940. They were nervous, and their friend recognized it immediately.

"What is it that troubles you, my children?" Padre asked.

Victoro and Gena glanced at each other, each waiting for the other to speak.

"Come now," the friar coaxed patiently, "nothing can be so bad as to make you fear speaking to me."

"It is not fear, Padre," Victoro finally said, "it is that we are uneasy about the fact that the Church has not spoken out against the horrors that occur right under our noses. We cannot believe that she condones these atrocities, but how else is the silence to be interpreted? We've come to ask two things of you, and we are afraid to put you into a compromising position."

"You've come first for my blessing, and secondly for my help. Well ask them of me then."

Both paled a little. "You knew all along?" Gena asked.

Pio nodded. "A parent senses when his children undertake a danger. Be careful. You have my blessing, and you will receive my help. Please say no more about it. At times like these, the less said the better. You take a risk. But what is not a risk these days? When we live among evil, all the good that we do is done at risk."

The couple left, not having gone into the matter with Padre Pio but having accomplished all they had hoped for.

"How do you think he will help?" Gena asked, as they walked down the road which had been widened and made less steep since the first time she had ascended it years earlier.

"Who knows? God works in strange ways, and so does Padre

Pio. But I am sure his help will come when it is most needed. I am satisfied that we have his blessing. That alone should keep us safe and assure our success."

When they arrived at the inn, two German staff cars were in front. Victoro smiled at the driver standing at the side of the first car. "Good morning, Hans, your colonel is not up yet?"

"Oh, he is up. He has a meeting in his room with another officer this morning," the driver said, nodding his head toward the second staff car parked behind his own.

There weren't a lot of Germans in the town. They were far more visible in the larger Italian cities. Very few were stationed in San Giovanni Rotondo, and those only because there was an airfield in the vicinity. **Colonel Zimmermann** came to San Giovanni Rotondo once a week and stayed one to three days, depending on what problems arose in the interim. He had a suite billeted in the inn. His driver also had a room there, and another room was assigned to **Sergeant Meisterling**. The sergeant was the colonel's aide and stayed all the time in San Giovanni Rotondo, stationed at the inn.

As Gena and Victoro walked past the second staff car, Victoro nodded a greeting to the second driver standing at the side of his vehicle. The German arrogantly ignored the gesture.

"Bastards," Victoro mumbled to Gena.

As they entered the inn, she replied, "I guess we're lucky at

that. The colonel and his aide and driver are at least polite and reasonable, but some of the Germans who come here to see them truly are bastards."

"Not some. Most."

Victoro checked around and saw that there were no Germans on the first floor of the inn. Only **Sophia** was around. Sophia was housekeeper, waitress, sometime cook, general helper around the inn, and was trusted by Victoro and Gena. Her sympathies were with them, and their risks were her's as well. Victoro went to her and whispered, "I am going downstairs. Buzz if anyone needs me, twice if anyone goes near the basement entrance."

She nodded. He went to the door on the other side of the eating area of the inn, through the small kitchen and to another door, which opened to a dark stairway. The only light for the stairs was that which slipped down from the dimly lit kitchen. Victoro took hold of the banister and groped his way down. At the bottom he reached overhead and felt at the darkness until he came in contact with a metal-beaded light chain. He grasped it and gave it a little pull. A naked, unshaded bulb came on. It hung from an electric wire from the ceiling, which consisted of the joists and flooring of the floor above. The little bulb threw only a small radius of light in the large basement that spread under the entire inn.

The floor was of flagstone, large red sandstone pieces, recently grouted with concrete. Victoro walked past the shelves of supplies, past the border of the dim light. Once again in darkness he felt along one wall until he found another switch. This one was on the wall, put in much later than the original hanging fixture. No one would ever be able to find it if he didn't know where to feel. No light reached this area. He flipped the switch, and another lamp, one with three bulbs, illuminated the rest of the basement. Though it wasn't overly bright in the basement, at least the three additional bulbs threw their dim light into all corners of the subterranean storage area.

At the far end of the basement, opposite from the stairs, the entire wall was shelved. Victoro went to the left end of the shelving, where the light was dimmer, and vanished.

Chapter 61

"Our best guess is that a munitions dump is located somewhere in this vicinity, General." **Captain Jack Gabriel** was circling a small area on the map with his finger. The Americans were now on Italian soil, and had an airbase located just outside **Bari.**

General Kenneth Derryberry studied the tattered map. "San Giovanni Rotondo..." he mumbled. "That's less than 100 miles from here. Any serious ground fire?"

"Our observation planes encountered none, sir. And the pilots have been unable to spot any artillery capable of giving us any trouble if we come from this direction." Captain Gabriel scratched a light, thin line with his pencil.

The General wanted to hear this. Piloting "big birds" was his love, but-because he had become a General before the United States had entered into war against Germany, he had yet to fly a mission. His expected place was on the ground, and for the past several months he had watched with envy as his troops lifted off the runway and disappeared into the skies. This is my chance, my turn!

"I will lead the raid," he said with a proud tone in his voice. "We'll strike at 0600."

It was a safe mission. Apple pie. The Captain was very perceptive, and sympathized with his commander. He would not argue, or even hint that the General was making an unwise decision. "Yes sir!"

The morning was perfect. The cool, crisp air splashed the face of General Kenneth Derryberry as he took long steps towards his plane. The squeaking of his leather flight jacket was music to his ears. He felt good. It was a small mission, but it was his mission. The engines coughed, then began their steady, familiar hum. The General looked over at his co-pilot, Captain **John "Scotty" Scott**, and smiled. "Let's go."

The shadows of five B-17s slipped over the rural countryside. As they neared the vicinity of San Giovanni Rotondo, the General reached down and pulled back the lever, which operated the bombay doors.

"Damn!" He looked up at the blinking red light on the instrument panel. The doors were not opening. Leaning over and grabbing the lever with both hands, he tried the procedure again, this time with more force. It was to no avail. "The sonof-a-bitch is jammed," grunted the General as he continued to struggle with the lever.

"HOLY SHIT!!!"

The co-pilot's high-pitched voice unnerved the General. In an instant he was sitting erect in his seat, both hands instinctively clasped tightly around the control wheel. Looking out the window in front of him, he expected to see a squadron of enemy fighter planes.

"I don't believe this! God, I really don't believe this! Holy shit!" rattled Scotty.

General Derryberry was dumbfounded. He gazed unbelievably at the sight ahead. The figure of a man, garbed in brown robes, was facing them, yet was moving backwards at the equal speed of the aircraft.

"It's a hundred feet tall! Holy shit! It's waving its arms like it wants us to turn around, General. What the hell we goin' to do?"

"Turn around," he mumbled. There is nothing else I can do. He ordered his planes back to base. On the way back, the planes would find an open area in which to drop the bombs, thus assuring a safe landing. The bombay doors on his own plane began to work again.

After he returned to the airbase, General Derryberry went directly to the Officer's Club, ordered a stiff drink, and sat down alone at a small table in the corner. When he had landed, none of the other pilots had mentioned seeing anything peculiar. Nor had they dared question him about the aborted mission.

He stared at his drink as he spun the glass around with his fingers. *Thank God my co-pilot saw the thing, too. The military would think me crazy. I'm still going to be asked a lot of questions, I'm sure. It's probably all over the base by nwo, Scotty will make sure of that!*

His thoughts were interrupted by the mention of his name.

"General Derryberry? May I join you, please?"

The General looked up to see an Italian officer standing beside him. He didn't know the fellow by name, but had seen him in the club on a few occasions. "Uh ... Sure ... Pull up a chair." Here it comes. He's got a strange look in his eyes. Maybe he's looking at me like that because he thinks I'm nuts. His new guest sat down anxiously.

The General leaned back in his chair and lit a cigarette, ready to defend himself. "What can I do for you, my friend?"

"I am told ... er ... I mean, I have heard ... that you saw something different this morning. Is this correct?"

The General leaned forward and rested his wrists on the edge of the table. "Now look, pal ... I don't know what you've heard, but…"

"Please. Save your anger. Is this the person you saw today?" The officer quickly placed a small photograph in front of the General as he stared at his face with anticipation.

The General lifted the photo from the table and held it closer. He studied it silently for a full minute before looking up at the officer. "Who is this?"

"Is that the man you saw?"

"Yes." The conviction in his voice brought a smile to the Italian's face.

"The photograph is that of Padre Pio, a monk who lives in a monastery situated above the town of San Giovanni Rotondo. The people there say that he is a saint. And I say he is a saint."

"Do you know him?"

"I think, General, I know him in the same sense that you do."

"Then ... you have seen him also?" Now it was the General who had the anxious look in the eyes.

"What I will tell you now, you will find almost unbelievable. I repeat this story to a select few, for someone might suspect me mad. Do you understand?"

"Too well."

"It happened about four months ago, in a temporary camp stationed approximately 30 miles south of here. I had just received news of my brother's death, and was in my tent trying to drown my sorrows with several bottles of wine. A soldier entered my quarters with another telegram. I opened it anxiously, hoping that it brought me news that the previous telegram had been a mistake, and that my young brother was still alive. We were very close, you know. But it was only more bad tidings, tidings, which pierced my heart like a white-hot blade. My father and mother had been killed during an air attack. Innocent! They were so innocent! Why them? Why should… " The Italian officer put his head down and covered his eyes with his hand. The General reached across the small table and laid his hand on the officer's shoulder.

"The monk," he said softly, "tell me about the monk."

The Italian regained his composure and sat erect in his chair. His eyes glanced around the immediate area of the room to see if any others had witnessed his moment of emotional weakness.

"In my drunken state I was not able to deal with this news. I ordered the courier from my tent and told the sentry stationed in front of my quarters that I was not to be disturbed. I sat down on my bed, drew my revolver from my holster, I pointed it into my mouth. Just as I began to squeeze the trigger, I was aware of another presence. Looking up, I saw a monk.

"'That is a foolish thing to do,' he said. And he touched my very soul with his words. I knew that I had much to do to help my fellow countrymen. They mattered much more than I. Immediately I became sober."

"He spoke to you? What else did he say?"

"No other words were spoken. They didn't need to be. His eyes ... they were so…can I think of the right words…so warm, so understanding. Then he disappeared. I went out of my tent and asked the sentry why he had disobeyed my orders, why he had allowed someone to enter. But he swore he had been standing there all the while, and that positively no one had even come close to my tent."

"How did you come to realize it was the monk in this picture?"

"That was very easy. As I said before, he is believed to be a saint in this country. There have been many other stories. Just as phenomenal. It wasn't difficult to find someone who carried his picture."

"How do you explain his being there at that precise moment?"

"General, it is common knowledge that this man has never left the walls of the monastery where he resides. Just as it is common knowledge with the residents of San Giovanni Rotondo that this monk promised that their countryside would never be bombed."

A faint smile crossed the General's lips. "Humph ... A saint you say. How about another drink, my friend, while you tell me more…"

Chapter 62

Solomon deSola's family had lived in Rome for almost two centuries. They'd migrated there from Naples. He could trace his forebears back to 1492, when they came to the Kingdom of Naples, refugees of the Spanish Inquisition. Now the Nazis had deported all of his family to a concentration camp in Germany. Only he had escaped the roundup of Jews in the ghetto section of Rome. It hadn't been a matter of skill or intelligence that kept him from being caught up in the mass arrest. It had been pure luck. He'd been with a Christian friend for two days in another part of the city. When he finally came home he saw that the streets around his home had been cordoned off. His first impulse had been to try to get in and go to the aid of his family, to be with them, but he quickly realized that if there were any hope of aiding them, he'd have to stay free.

He hung back in the crowd of people gathering to watch the arrest of all the Jews. They were dragged out of their homes, lined up in the streets, and then put on trucks at gunpoint and under the intimidation of guard dogs. Two or three tried to resist and were shot at point-blank range. That shocked the rest of the crowd into submission. Children and women cried. The men stood helplessly by, separated from their families, watching their wives, children and elderly being loaded on different trucks from their own.

"There is another Jew, I recognize him," someone in the crowd yelled. "He is a Jew. Don't let him get away."

Solomon turned toward the sound, as did the rest of the crowd. He was terrified to see the accuser pointing at him as he called attention to the Germans.

Frightened, Solomon bounded from the crowd and started running. Two Germans tried to chase him but were slowed by the congestion of spectators.

"Let us through! Step aside, let us through. Stop that Jew…"

A number of the Italians actually closed ranks, pretending confusion, preventing the soldiers from giving chase. Solomon ran until his legs would no longer carry him.

He ran blindly, fear-driven. When he finally stopped he was in a section outside the ghetto. He was vaguely familiar with the area. Stepping into a doorway, he looked back in the direction from which he had run. He watched a long while. *No one's following me. God, what do I do now? I'll go back to Toni's. They'll help me. Maybe they can help me find out about mama, papa, the rest of my family.*

He went back to his friend's home and told Toni and his family what had happened.

"You stay here," Toni's father said, "inside the house. Stay off the streets. I'll go to the Gestapo Headquarters and see if I can find anything out."

Both Toni and Solomon were eighteen. They had been in their first year of college when the Germans came to Rome.

Because of their influence, all Jews were forced to drop out of school. Since that time, Solomon had tried to find work, but for Jews there was none.

Solomon had black hair, olive skin, was wiry, and just less than six feet tall. He had deep brown eyes. Before the war he had a perpetual smile on his face, but these were not smiling times. He looked like any other Italian. Often he thought about trying to pass for a Christian to get work, but to get a false identity card was punishable by imprisonment or even death. He'd not yet been desperate enough for that.

Several hours passed before Toni's father returned. "I couldn't find out a thing at Gestapo Headquarters, couldn't even get in. So I went over to your neighborhood. There's lots of talk there. Several people followed the trucks." Toni's father became silent a moment, his expression stern, "I'm sorry, Solomon, they went straight to the freight yards and loaded them on to trains. No one knows where they've been sent. I can't think of any way you or anyone else can help."

Solomon's head hung. He looked down at his lap. Tears filled his eyes. He whimpered helplessly. "What shall I do now? Oh God, what shall I do?"

"You'll stay here tonight," Toni's father said. "No one knows you're here. You'll be safe for the time being. We'll have to figure out how to get you out of the country. There are too many who would turn you over to the Nazis for some favor. Just like that voice in the crowd you told us about today. We can trust no one." He looked at Tony and his mother, "We must tell no one that Solomon is here. No one!"

Chapter 63

Victoro was in a room about thirty feet long and fifteen feet wide. He was giving it a last-minute inspection. The ceiling was covered with boards screwed to the joists of the floor above. The spaces between the boards and the flooring above had been stuffed with rags, newspapers, sawdust, old clothes; anything that might help to soundproof the chamber. There were no windows, but four strong electric bulbs illuminated the room much more brightly than the basement. All the walls were lined with shelves packed with supplies, many more than the basement had held for the operation of the inn. There were no fewer than eight cots, and a small table and five chairs were in one corner. The opposite corner held a chamber pot hidden by a screen. One shelf held several volumes, among them an Old Testament; after all, this place would be occupied by **the people of the Book.**

The floor was the same flagstone as the basement. Everything looked ready. He looked up at the ceiling. He heard no sounds from upstairs. He hoped that sound would not travel in the other direction either, but then he'd tested that. He had Gena and Sophia speak loudly in the room while he listened upstairs. He looked at the hundreds of screws he had driven to hold up the ceiling. "What a horrible job that was, but I couldn't risk the noise of hammering," he mumbled to himself.

Satisfied, he returned to the corner where he had entered. He pulled open a section of wall. As it swung into the room, it revealed shelves on the other side. Victoro let himself out, leaving the lights on in the room. He pulled the door shut behind him, as he stepped back into the dim light of his inn's basement.

He went to the switch on the wall and flipped it off. He went to the light with the pull chain, yanked it and left the basement in darkness. Then he went back toward the wall he'd come through. Carefully, he looked in its direction through the darkness. "Black," he murmured, "not a speck of light shows through."

Returning to the chain, he turned on the hanging light, made his way back to the wall switch, went to the secret door, reopened it, and turned off the lights in the secret room. He headed back to the stairs, turned off all the other lights in order, and went up, locking the basement door behind him in the kitchen. A smile was on his face, the smile of a man satisfied with a job well done.

Chapter 64

It was decided that Solomon should get out of Rome. The heaviest concentration of Germans was in the largest cities, also the largest number of Nazi sympathizers. Toni's father and the two boys decided that Solomon would have his best chance in the country or even in the mountains. Toni's father had a car; they would drive into the country on the weekend. Toni had an uncle who owned land. Perhaps they could hide Solomon as a farm laborer, at least temporarily, until further plans could be made. On Sunday they drove to the Southeast, toward the coast.

"What do you know about grapes?" Toni's father asked.

"Who, me?" Solomon asked.

"Yes you."

"Not much. You make wine out of them. They grow on vines. They're good to eat. Why?"

"It's a vineyard you're going to. You'll know a lot more about them soon. We'll try to get you on there as hired help. I think you'll be safe there, but be on your guard at all times."

Toni's uncle, **Roberto**, was willing to help. "Don't worry, we'll keep him safe here. We haven't even seen a German in these parts. I'll put you to work in the vineyards. In a few days no one will know you from any of the other hands.

"Then we'll see about smuggling you out of the country. I don't know anyone who smuggles people, but I know plenty of people who smuggle everything else."

"But you have to be careful, Uncle Roberto," Toni warned, "you can't just ask anyone. You could get reported yourself for soliciting such help."

"He's right," Toni's father agreed. "You just don't know who might be in sympathy with the Germans. These are dangerous times."

Solomon had been quietly listening, but now he felt he had to speak, "I can't let you take such risks. It is enough that you give me a place to stay and work. Please, let me try to find my own way out. That will reduce the chance you take. If I do get caught, then you can always claim you knew nothing about it. If you ask around for me, you'll implicate yourself. Please, I insist. I'll find a way."

"Well, we'll see, " Roberto said. "In the meantime you'll work for me and live here on the property."

They showed Solomon his room and bed. He bid Toni and his father goodbye and returned to his room to worry over his deported family.

Chapter 65

Several weeks passed. The room in the basement of the inn still stood empty. Victoro and his two conspirators were getting impatient.

"How will anyone know to come here?" Sophia asked. "The room will never be used. Whom will we help?"

"It will be used," Victoro replied. "Just as I knew to build it, they will know to come here for help."

"What did make you build it?" Gena asked.

Victoro smiled, "You'll really think me crazy, but I just awoke one morning and knew I had to build that room. I knew just how to do it, as if it had been planned for me."

"Had you dreamed about it?" Sophia asked.

"If I did, I didn't remember. It was just something I knew I had to do."

Sophia looked at him questioningly. "I'm still afraid the room will never be used."

"Be patient, Sophia," Victoro replied. "The war will be long. It is not the kind of service we can advertise. Give it time."

"And what will we do once they are here, Victoro?" Gena asked. "They can't spend the duration in our basement."

"Oh, they could, but I'm confident they won't have to." His companions did not share Victoro's confidence.

Another three weeks passed. The room still stood empty. Sophia brought Victoro and Gena breakfast in the dining area. Colonel Zimmermann sat at a table across the room, by a window, reading a German newspaper. Sophia was nervous and irritable this morning. As she was serving coffee to her employers, she finally whispered, "Do you think it wise that we do what we've planned when Germans live under the same roof with us?"

"What better place than right under their noses?" Victoro replied. "It is the last place they would suspect, the last place they would search."

Sophia remained uneasy.

Victoro had to go out to buy vegetables that morning. Supplies were getting scarce in Italy, and food lines were getting longer throughout the country. One of the advantages of having a colonel billeted at the inn was that Victoro didn't have to stand in lines, and he got better selections of the foods. Much of what he bought went into the secret room.

As he was returning from the market, a youth of about eighteen approached Victoro. "I beg your pardon sir, but are you the man who runs the inn at the edge of town?"

"Yes, I own the inn."

"You are the man called Victoro?" the youth asked. "Yes. How can I help you?"

"I was told to ask you about a special room." The young man went on to describe the room perfectly. Victoro was clearly shocked by the description.

"How do you know me? Who sent you?" Thoughts raced wildly through Victoro's head. He tried to keep his composure. *Who could have told him about that room? It's as if he has seen it. Could it be a trick? What do I say to him? How can I be sure about him? Why didn't I plan for this?*

"You were described to me by a monk. He told me exactly what you would be wearing and when you would walk past here carrying those sacks of food."

"What monk? Where?"

"He came to me two days ago at the vineyard where I was working. He told me exactly how to get here, described you, told me to describe the room so you would know my needs."

Victoro interrupted, "Describe the monk."

"He wore a brown robe with a hood. He had a white rope as a belt. He must have injured himself because he had bandages on both hands and feet. He wore sandals. The most peculiar thing was that he wore a perfume. I didn't know monks used perfume."

Victoro had no more doubts. "Hide yourself in the woods beyond the fields on the other side of the inn. I will get you tonight after dark. You will be safe. By the way, what is your name?"

"Solomon. Solomon deSola."

Over the next three weeks, five more Jewish refugees came to the inn from all parts of Italy, all with the same story, that a monk had given them instructions on how to reach the inn, recognize the owner, and describe the room they wanted.

Victoro was still waiting for some sign of what to do next.

Three days after the fifth refugee came to the inn, a burly, peasantly looking man approached Victoro outside the inn. "I am told you are the man called Victoro, owner of this inn."

"That's right. And who might you be?"

"In my line I'd just as soon not give my name. It should be enough to tell you that the friar-priest sent me to you. I understand you have some passengers for me, six altogether."

He gave Victoro full instructions, and two days later the basement room was again empty.

Victoro's inn was now an important part of a network to help refugees, both religious and political, out of the country. They came to him for the duration of the war. He hid them safely until their transportation out of the country was scheduled. The Germans billeted at the inn never suspected what went on in the basement, nor did the people of San Giovanni Rotondo. It was a secret between Victoro and Padre Pio, how such an intricate, underground escape network could have just come together on its own. "It is truly a miracle," Victoro used to say. He wasn't joking.

Chapter 66

Nothing grieved Padre Pio more than the suffering of the thousands of sick that came to him each year. It was a constant frustration to him that so little could be done for them. Not because their cases were hopeless, but because of the lack of facilities available to them. Those who's cases were hopeless he could help with comfort, faith, prayer, and sometimes with miracles. But there were tens of thousands who needed only medical help for their pains and sufferings. Doctors, facilities, and funds for their care were just not sufficient. Padre Pio's dream was to build a "tabernacle of healing," a hospital so magnificent that it could take in those who needed medical help, regardless of their affliction and their ability to pay.

In 1939 he began planning in earnest. He called together several influential men of the community and told them what he had in mind. They all admired his intentions but pointed out the impracticality of the plan. "To build such a hospital would cost a fortune. We'd never be able to raise the money."

"To staff such a place would be a tremendous problem. Doctors, nurses, technicians would have to be brought into San Giovanni Rotondo by the hundreds."

"To build what you envision would be an engineering feat unheard of."

The Capuchin listened to all of their doubts, then said, "It will be done."

He appointed a committee to set the wheels in motion, and then World War II began. That ended any hope of starting construction or even raising funds. The dream had to be tabled for the duration. But the dream grew, and the Padre continued his own planning. "Everything has its time and place. When its time comes I will be ready."

A second meeting was called six years later. Before the war, about $6,000 had been collected in the form of contributions, but postwar inflation had cut its value to the equivalent of about 75 prewar dollars. They would have to start from scratch. Padre Pio was determined to have his **Casa Sollievo Della Sofferenza...Home for the Relief of Suffering.**

Those men at the meeting who had doubted the feasibility of the project in 1939 were now shocked to find that in the six-year interim the plans had become even more grandiose. They agreed to work along with Padre Pio, more to humor him than because they had any hope for success.

Contributions started to pour in as Padre Pio appealed to all those who came to Saint Mary of the Graces. They took the appeal back to their homes, and money started to come in by mail. Newspapers and magazines picked up the story, and more funds arrived. In 1946, an English author became intrigued by the project. Her name was **Miss Barbara Ward**. Her work had made her a close acquaintance of **Feorello LaGuardia**, the **past Mayor of New York City.** She knew that his family had come from the region of Foggia. He was familiar with the poverty of Southern

Italy, sympathetic with the people who lived there. He was also director general of **UNRRA**. Feorello LaGuardia was so moved by Padre Pio's concept that he arranged a grant of almost $350,000 of UNRRA funds. For his help, the clinic at the Home for the Relief of Suffering would be named the **Feorello LaGuardia Clinic**.

Now that the dream was to become a reality, Padre Pio made a strange decision. Of all the experienced hospital architects and engineers in the world, he chose none. Instead, he gave the job of designing and building his hospital to a man who didn't even have a degree, a self-taught man with only an elementary-school education, **Angelo Lupi.**

Angelo was himself surprised when he was appointed to the job. "Padre Pio, I do not have an architectural or engineering degree," he pointed out. "For a job like this I think you would want someone formally trained. I am not. Are you sure you don't want to reconsider?"

"Angelo, I have talked with the others. All they do is tell me what we want has never been done before, that it is impossible, that it is too big, that it is not the usual. I'm hoping you have not learned what is impossible. God does not give us impossible tasks to do, only difficult projects. I've talked with you often enough over the years about this dream. Do you consider it impossible?"

"It is not impossible."

"That, Angelo, is why you have been chosen. There will be problems, but each problem will have a solution, probably several solutions. I am confident that when the problems arise, you will find the best solution. When all the solutions have been found, we will have our Home for the Relief of Suffering."

Like the monastery, the hospital was to be built into the side of the mountain. The first task then was to cut away a large section of the mountainside. For that, enormous equipment was needed. To buy or lease such equipment would take almost all the money collected thus far. Angelo suggested the solution to this first problem.

"Southern Italy has never had enough work for its people. Why do we not save some of the money needed for heavy equipment and give jobs to laborers to do the work in the old ways? We can give work to thousands and feed many empty stomachs. We will get only the most necessary heavy equipment. Also, we will buy only raw material and make what we need here on the job whenever we can. From the rock we dig out of the mountain we can make our own gravel. We can cut our own stones, make our own concrete. We will bring in raw lumber and hire carpenters to build scaffolding, furniture, cabinets, everything wooden, right here. That will put more needy people to work, and it will save us money."

These ideas were revolutionary. They were not progressive, modern. Angelo was not following the lead of the rest of the mechanized world. The directors of the project were skeptical.

"The man is not rational. This is the twentieth century. His ways are obsolete. We are making a great mistake by not using someone with experience," they agreed.

Padre Pio disagreed. "The Great Wall of China was a much bigger job. It was done with the labor of tens of thousands. Their tools were far more primitive. I doubt that today's engineers or builders would tackle the task today, even with their new methods. Angelo's ideas fit our needs. We will follow his lead." The decision was made.

Within days, desperate people flocked to the site looking for work. It was the first chance of employment in years for most of them. They were eager to work, grateful for the opportunity. With picks and shovels they started to cut away at the mountain. In the early morning, blasting could be heard. It echoed through the entire mountain range. The rest of the day workers cleared the rubble. To everyone's' surprise but Padre Pio's and Angelo's, the work progressed quickly.

Angelo built a limekiln on the premises, and from the stone they dug out he was able to make plaster. He hired people to make bathtubs, sinks, tiles and composition paneling right on the site. He began to impress all of his previous doubters. Others were also impressed. People in high places, government agencies, took notice. Finding work for the unemployed was a major problem in the postwar economy. Suddenly, government and war-rehabilitation money became available. Not only had Angelo saved money for the project, he had accidently tapped a new source.

But his ingenuity didn't stop there. Water on the site was short. Drilling for more was prohibitive in cost, and the chance of finding only an inadequate supply was too great. But water was necessary to life and project. As every solution was ruled out, Angelo again reached back to ancient times for the answer. He constructed a tie-in to the **Aqueduct of Apulia**. Like the ancient Romans, he built giant cisterns to collect rainwater and runoff from the mountain. He also built a power plant for the project and future hospital.

By September of 1946, enough of the mountain had been cut away. The foundation could now be started. As he watched his dream coming true, Padre Pio would have said these were the happiest days of his life. But his joy was not to be unblemished. On October 7th, 1946, his father Orazio died after a short illness. The hundreds of friends he'd made while he lived in San Giovanni Rotondo attended his funeral. He was laid to rest next to his wife Maria Giuseppe, who'd died several years before. Among the mourners were five great-grandchildren, the sons and daughters of Padre Pio's older brother Michele's daughter.

Padre Pio was deeply depressed by the loss. "How often the Lord has worked his wonders through me, to relieve illness in others," he said to one of the Brothers, "but when it came to my own parents I could only sit helplessly by as they passed on."

It was not difficult to notice that as Padre Pio's depression deepened, Angelo's ability to solve the everyday problems and his talent for creation decreased. Then one morning he was up early and had a solution for every obstacle that had arisen over the past few days. Padre Pio had prayed the entire night before to overcome his deep grief. He, too, found himself fresh of mind and with a renewed vigor that morning.

As work on the clinic progressed, Angelo's devotion to his work deepened. He was up long before dawn, worked late into the night, took no time off. He supervised and inspected every aspect of the construction, seemed to know every nail and screw in the rising structure. Some thought him possessed.

When those who observed pointed out to Padre Pio that they thought Angelo should take some time off, Padre Pio replied, "He knows he is welcome to take off anytime he wishes, but I know he will not rest until the job is done. His schedule is beyond our control."

Angelo did take a day of rest. It was just after Easter of 1947. All work ceased for a ceremony to lay the cornerstone of the actual clinic building. The next morning he was back on the site before dawn. For three and a half years, Angelo worked without another day off. Each day he would inspect the previous day's work before the workmen arrived for that day's labor. As each day passed, his energy and confidence seemed to strengthen. He was tireless. No challenge frightened him. When a more difficult problem did arise, he would stand before the project and look up at a window of the monastery. In a short while, Padre Pio would appear in that window. Their eyes would meet. Not a word was spoken, but soon a smile would creep over Angelo's face and he would cross himself, as would Padre Pio, and the architect would go back into the structure, his problem solved.

On October 7th, 1949, Angelo Lupi did not show up to work.

During that night, Padre Pio had taken ill. No one outside the monastery knew about the illness, but Angelo could not bring himself to come to work. He himself was not ill. "I just cannot bring myself to do any work. I have no ideas. I can't even think about the problems. My mind is a blank. Please ask Padre Pio to forgive me." He had no knowledge of the Capuchin's illness.

Padre Pio developed a severe respiratory illness with extremely high fever. He was bedridden, seriously ill. On the second day, Angelo came to the building site, but he just wandered around the construction, unable to make his usual brilliant contribution. He went outside and sat down on a drum, and looked up at the window, but Padre Pio did not appear.

The doctors and Brothers were very concerned. Two days, three days, a week went by, and there was no improvement. His fevers spiked to temperatures of one hundred and twenty. Work on the hospital came almost to a standstill without the guidance of Angelo Lupi. When his foremen asked him to help them he could only answer, "Without the guidance of God, further work on the Home for the Relief of Suffering cannot go on."

Workmen finished what work they could, and then they sat down and kept a vigil on the little window. Finally, after ten days, Angelo came to the site with a bounce in his step. He positioned himself before the window and waited for the familiar face that only he knew would make its appearance that day. During that night Padre Pio's fever broke. In the morning he felt well and hungry. On his way to Mass he stopped at the window and looked down on his protégé. For a long while they stared at each other. Silence hung over the gathering workers. Then Padre Pio left the window. Angelo looked about at the workers, "All right everyone, let's get back to work; we've already lost too much time!"

On December 9th, 1949, another short ceremony was

held.

The roof over the Feorello LaGuardia Clinic was completed. Donations kept pouring in. Expenditures were high. It constantly appeared that the project would run out of money, and everyone would worry, except Padre Pio. Each time he would say, "The Lord shall provide," and each time more funds would come in from some new, untapped source.

ꕤ ꕤ ꕤ ꕤ

Six more years the construction went on, then, just before Christmas of 1955, the Home for the Relief of Suffering was finished. Now Angelo Lupi could take his long-earned rest. Padre Pio's first words to him were, "It is a magnificent work you have done; an act of true love and charity. Angelo, you have now earned your degree."

Dignitaries from all over the world came to San Giovanni Rotondo for the dedication of Padre Pio's Home for the Relief of Suffering. What they found when they arrived was a palace of healing. "This is how it must have felt to the first people who saw the Taj Mahal when it was first completed. This place is magnificent," one of the honored guests was heard to say.

One hundred and fifty windows opened out of the front of the four-story clinic building. It was built entirely of pink cut stone. The patients who would use the hospital would have a view of the valley below, and then the fields clear to the sea. Five hundred beds were ready to be occupied. There was not a ward in the building. No more than four patients would be put into any room. The building was completely air-conditioned, almost unheard of in Italy in that day. The surgical suites were as modern as any in the world. There were also special operating rooms on the second floor for minor and outpatient procedures. A library boasted the latest in medical books and publications, as well as a section of current and classical works for the benefit of the patients. Radiology had the latest in diagnostic and therapeutic equipment. The laboratory was second to none in all Europe. The pharmacy was stocked with the latest in drugs. There was even a motion picture theater on the premises.

The third floor housed a modern internal medicine and cardiology department. The fourth floor was for obstetrics and pediatrics. Surgery patients were on the second floor. Rooms were airy and bright and with a homey rather than clinical look.

There was a center for nurses' training and for interns. Education of personnel to practice the finest medicine in the world was an important goal of the institution. Twenty-four doctors, more than eighty nurse, and hundreds of technicians were ready to receive their first patients.

Halls and rooms were floored in tile. Stairways and pillars were of the finest marble. And there was a magnificent chapel available to staff and patients. Altogether, the structure had been built for less than five million dollars; itself a miracle.

Chapter 67

All of his adult life, Padre Pio had prayed for his own death. He saw it as his only hope for peace, escape from the torment of demons, from witnessing the suffering on earth, from his own pain. But as long as God had work for him in life he would dedicate all his energy to the betterment of man.

After he saw the fulfillment of his dream, the completion of the Home for the Relief of Suffering, he'd hoped that his term on earth might be drawing to a close. But it wasn't. His workload grew. The number of pilgrims that came to Saint Mary of the Graces multiplied year by year. He served Mass, spent long hours in the confession booth, sometimes well past ten at night, performed miracles at San Giovanni Rotondo as well as around the world with bilocation, met in private conferences with rich and poor alike, and supervised the operation of the Home for the Relief of Suffering. And all during that time he was constantly being tested by the tormenting demons.

Not until1959 was he given, at least, the promise of his long-awaited rest.

He was sitting in the garden with a group of Brothers. Their talk had been casual. The sun was settling behind the west wall, and a cooling breeze had sprung up from the sea. It was the time of day that flowers begin to close their petals. It was a good time for the friars to take a break from their heavy chores.

Padre Pio was entertaining his companions with witty tales, as he often did. Suddenly he stopped in mid-sentence. He stared directly at an area of the garden about ten feet away. He became absorbed…

"Are you all right, Padre?" one of the younger friars asked.

"Shhhh," Brother Carmelo hushed the younger priest, "He'll not hear you."

The friars watched Pio in silence as tears began to well up in his eyes. At the same time he smiled faintly. Once he seemed to mouth words, but no one could make out what might have been said. The fragrance of flowers became stronger. One and then another of the Brothers bowed their heads in silent meditation. In less than two minutes, Padre Pio's attention came back to his earthly friends, but he did not continue his story. He looked about at his gathered Brothers and said, tears still in his eyes, "I will have to bear the stigmata for no less than fifty years. I will not be called to my Heavenly peace until my eighty-second year. Not until after the blessing of my crypt."

Nothing further was said. Padre Pio arose and shuffled toward the chapel.

This prophecy was a great relief to the Brothers. The new church in Pietrelcina that Padre Pio had foreseen as a child was to be dedicated soon, on the very spot where he'd told the archpriest, Don Salvatore Pannullo, that he heard church bells ringing. There had been some speculation and fear that the dedication of that church might be an omen of the Capuchin's death.

In 1965, Padre Pio's health began to deteriorate. Until then, he still worked fifteen, sometimes twenty hours every day. But he was beginning to have more frequent flare ups of respiratory disease, and his recovery from each was not as complete as before. He frequently was too weak to leave his cell, and he spent his days praying in his own cubical.

Just about the time his physicians felt his illness was terminal, he would make a sudden recovery and return to full days of work, serving Mass, hearing hours of confessions, performing weddings, baptisms, blessing the dead, and intervening for those who had lost all hope by performing miracles.

When his doctors expressed their fears and implored him to slow his pace, he merely answered, "Save your fears for others; my fate is sealed. I must bear the stigmata for at least fifty years. My rest cannot come before September 20th of 1968.

On July 7th of 1968 he suffered his worst flare-up the lung disease that had plagued his entire life. It was complicated by a full-blown asthma attack.

This illness lasted several weeks. He was assigned to a new and larger cell, six feet by eighteen feet. It was luxury he had never known before. There were two windows that overlooked the garden.

An intercommunication system was put in so that the Brothers could monitor his every need, in or out of the room. During the long days, the friars took turns being available, staying with him, but much of the time he preferred to be alone.

Upon entering the cell, a small armchair, one Padre had learned to love, stood to the right. At its side was his little writing table. Two things that always were atop the table were his Rosary and some candy he had available for the children that came to see him. Usually it also held his tiny magnesia snuffbox, old and well worn.

His bed was opposite the door, a crucifix at its head. At the side of the bed hung a picture of Jesus being taken down from the Cross. On the north wall of the room hung numerous pictures of saints and many of his friends, including one of Angelo Lupi. Pictures of his parents hung on that wall surrounded by olive branches. There was one lamp in the room, on an end table. It also held an array of other items; a letter opener, his comb, an old Westclox alarm clock, a fountain pen or two, and a hearing aid which he seldom used. Books were usually strewn about the room.

Though he made only a partial recovery in July, he did return to his work. He served Mass and spent several hours in the confessional booth when able. But as his strength waned, he spent more and more time in his cell or on a small balcony he loved when the weather was sunny and warm, or in the garden. There he meditated and prayed, read and met with people who needed him. Often he had to be taken from one place to another by wheelchair. But at all times his mind stayed agile and alert. At last he was finding some peace, solitude and comfort on earth.

Chapter 68

Thousands of people came to San Giovanni Rotondo to celebrate the fiftieth anniversary of the stigmata. Priests from all over the world met that week in the little mountain town. The Vatican was represented. Capuchins came from as far away as the United States. Pilgrims swarmed to Saint Mary of the Graces.

Friday September 20th was the fiftieth anniversary day of the Capuchin's stigmata. The altar of the church was almost hidden by fifty vases of red roses given by some of his spiritual children. The church was filled to capacity when Padre Pio offered the Mass at his usual time, 5 a.m. To the people on the altar and in the front rows of the sanctuary, the wounds of his hands and feet were clearly visible. That afternoon he participated in the services, the recitation of the Rosary and Benediction of the Blessed Sacrament. At the completion of the services his fatigue was evident.

All day long, well-wishers congratulated him. He found genuine pleasure from the hundreds of messages from those who could not come to the celebration. He was deeply moved by the outpouring of love toward him.

That night he had another asthma attack, but it passed with treatment, and without lasting harm.

Saturday September 21st he awoke at the usual early hours of the morning but was too weak to offer Mass. At 5 a.m. he had another asthma attack. His lips turned blue, and his heart raced furiously. He perspired profusely, and his blood pressure dropped. Dr. Salas noticed that the bleeding of his stigmata had almost completely stopped.

He responded to treatment and later that morning was able to sit on his favorite veranda and pray and enjoy visiting with friends. He seemed less troubled by the usual pain of his wounds.

That afternoon he was able to attend the services, as he had the day before. That evening he spent in his room at prayer.

Sunday September 22nd Padre Pio awoke feeling weak again. He didn't think himself strong enough to offer Mass, but Brother Carmelo registered disappointment, and so he forced himself. Padre Pio walked to the altar with almost youthful steps. He had lost the shuffle that was a response to the terrible pain in his stigmatized feet. He sang the Mass that morning, clearly, loudly, beautifully. He was inspirational as never before. He coughed occasionally, but that was not unusual. He also gave First Holy Communion to one boy and two girls. He blessed all the congregation, tears in his eyes, a knowing smile on his face, then collapsed into the arms of two priests who had remained at his side.

Those congregated gasped, but in a few moments he recovered. For the first time a wheelchair was brought out to the altar. As he was being wheeled off to his room, he turned and looked back at the people. He stretched out his arms to them and called out, "My children, my children."

Later in the morning, his strength renewed, he went to the sacristy and made his thanksgiving. He wanted to go into the church to hear confessions but was not strong enough. He stopped at a window and blessed the crowd below. Before noon he regained enough strength to hear a few confessions. He spoke to a few women who approached him in the church, "I love everyone equally, but unfortunately, I am not received kindly by everyone." The women wept with him, and they prayed together.

Chapter 69

Padre Pio ate no lunch that day, only tasted the food brought to him. At 1 p.m. he lay down to rest. When the bell rang at 4:30 p.m. for the Benediction of the Blessed Sacrament, he responded immediately and remained through the entire service.

After the service, Padre Pio again stopped at the window and blessed the people who waited in the piazza below. He retired early.

At 9 that evening he called Padre Pellegrino on the intercom. When the friar came in, Padre Pio asked, "What time is it?"

"Just after 9. Is there anything you need? Anything I can do for you?"

"No, dear friend, I only needed to know the time."

Six times more that evening Padre Pio called in Padre Pellegrino just to ask the time. Each time the Capuchin's eyes were red from crying.

At 10 a.m. of the 22nd of September, **Padre Clemente, a Definitor General from Rome…**had blessed the crypt intended as a final resting place for the Capuchin.

Monday September 23rd, Padre Pio called Padre Pellegrino once more, at midnight. "My son, did you offer Mass yet?"

"Padre Pio, it is only a little after midnight. It is too early for Mass."

"Well, then you will have to offer it for me this morning."

He insisted on making his confession, adding, "My son, when the Lord calls me today, ask the Brothers to forgive me for all the trouble I have caused them. And ask my brethren and my spiritual children to pray for my soul."

Padre Pellegrino tried to answer but could not get the words out through the choking feeling in his throat. Tears ran down his cheeks into his Capuchin beard. At last he forced out the words with a wavering voice, "Father, I am sure the Lord will let you live a long time yet, but if you are right, may I ask for a last blessing for the brethren, for the spiritual children, and for your patients?"

"Yes, my Brother, I bless them all. Ask the superior to give them this last blessing for me."

He repeated his vows again, as he had when he was first ordained, vows that he had kept faithfully for all those years. Padre Pellegrino answered with the words, "And I, on the part of God, if you have observed these things, promise you everlasting life."

At Padre Pio's request, Padre Pellegrino remained at his side. At 1:30 a.m. Padre Pio sprang from his bed. He quickly changed from his pajamas to his Franciscan robes. Padre Pellegrino watched in awe as Pio slipped into his sandals. For years he had watched Pio painfully shuffle about on his wounded feet, but now the 82 year-old monk had the bounce of a young boy.

"Let us go to the sun parlor," said Pio.

Padre Pellegrino took his place behind the empty wheelchair and gave Pio a questioning glance. But Pio only smiled and passed him with painless steps. Pellegrino followed.

Pio snapped the switch, which lit the parlor. He sat himself in the chair from which he had greeted thousands upon thousands of guests over the years. His eyes surveyed the empty room for several minutes. Looking up at Padre Pellegrino, he said, "I shall miss my children. I think that is what I will miss most." He stood and returned to his cell.

The previous burst of energy was now gone. As he fell back into his armchair, it was evident his last bit of strength was drained. The Capuchin leaned back, his eyes closed, resting, waiting. He took a deep breath, savoring it, then another. Finally comfortable, his eyes opened. A smile came to his face. "I see my two mothers!" A pallor spread over him. Perspiration beaded on his brow. He now labored for each breath. His lips turned blue, purple. "**Gesu, Mari…Gesu, Maria**"…he kept repeating. His voice weakened.

Padre Pellegrino went for help. He called for Dr. Salas and got **Brother Bill Martin**. Brother Martin, who would later take the name **Father Giuseppe Pio**, helped place Pio on his bed. Within ten minutes, Dr. Salas arrived. The Capuchin responded momentarily to treatment.

They moved him back to his armchair because he could breathe easier sitting up. Two more physicians arrived. The other friars began gathering in the cell and the corridor. Padre Paolo administered the Sacrament of the Anointing of the Sick. The other Capuchins recited prayers for the dying.

Padre Pio pushed away the oxygen, bent his head slightly to the left, and closed his eyes.

"Padre! Padre!" Dr. Salas shouted.

The Capuchin opened his eyes, looked at the doctor with an expression reminiscent of someone saying good-bye to leave on a long anticipated journey, and then closed his eyes again, for the last time.

According to Dr. Gusso, "*Clinical signs of death, the most peaceful and sweet I have ever seen, were present at half past two.*"

Chapter 70

Everyone but Dr. Salas, Padres Carmelo and Pellegrino and three friars left the room. These stayed to prepare the body for final rest. As they began to wash the Capuchin, they were struck with awe.

"We are witnessing a true miracle," Dr. Salas whispered. Before their eyes Pio's wounds were healing. In a matter of minutes, the wounds had closed into scabs, and only moments later the scabs detached themselves from the body. The doctor examined the hands, feet, and chest. The skin was perfect, like that of a child's. There was no wound, no scab, no discoloration, no scar to be seen.

Brother Pellegrino, who had stood silent until now, spoke.

"Now I know the meaning of his words, 'I will die healthy'. It has happened just as he predicted."

Brother Carmelo recalled, "Over nine years ago he predicted his death, almost to the day. He told us, there in the garden, that he would not die until he had worn the stigmata for fifty years, not until after the blessing of his crypt. I heard it that day in the garden, after his vision, 'Not until after September 20th of 1968,' he told us, could he rest."

It was Sunday, September 23rd, 1968, and almost time for morning Mass.

Chapter 71

More than 100,000 people lined the mile-and-a-half funeral route. On September 26th, 1968, Padre Pio of Pietrelcina, the stigmatized Capuchin, was laid to rest in his crypt, under the sanctuary of the church he so loved. There he awaits Sainthood. The pilgrims still flock to him by the hundreds of thousands. And his miracles still continue.

"I will station myself at the gates of Paradise. I will not enter until all of my spiritual children have entered."

-Padre Pio

Epilogue

In 1982, the Vatican authorized **the Archbishop of Manfredonia** to open the investigation to discover whether Padre Pio should indeed be considered for sainthood. The investigation continued for seven years.

In 1989 it was deemed Padre Pio should progress to canonization.

Beginning in 1990, **the Congregation for the Causes of Saints** began debate as to how heroically Padre Pio had lived his life, and seven years later, in 1997 **Pope John Paul II declared him venerable.**

A discussion of the effects of Padre Pio's life on others followed, including the cure of an Italian woman, **Consiglia de Martino,** which had been associated with Padre Pio's intercession.

In 1999, on the advice of the Congregation, **John Paul II declared Padre Pio a personage blessed.**

There followed further consideration of Padre Pio's virtues and ability to do good even after his death, including discussion of other healings attributed to his intercession, the **Pope declared Padre Pio a saint on 16 June 2002.**

Well over three hundred thousand people were estimated to have attended the canonization ceremony.

On 1 July 2004, Pope John Paul II dedicated the Padre Pio Pilgrimage Church in San Giovanni Rotondo to the memory of Saint Pio of Pietrelcina.

Padre Pio has become one of the world's most popular saints. More Italian Catholics pray to Padre Pio than to any other figure.

ꟹ ꟹ ꟹ ꟹ

On 3 March 2008, the body of Saint Pio was exhumed from his crypt. Archbishop D'Ambrosio confirmed in a communiqué "**the stigmata are not visible**." He went on to say that St. Pio's hands "looked like they had just undergone a manicure.

Cardinal José Saraiva Martins, prefect for the Congregation for the Causes of the Saints, celebrated the Mass for 15,000 devotees on 24 April at the Shrine of Holy Mary of Grace, San Giovanni Rotondo, aftwr which the body went on display in a crystal, marble, and silver sepulcher in the crypt of the monastery.

Padre Pio is in repose wearing his brown Capuchin habit with its white silk stole embroidered with crystals and gold thread. His hands are holding a large wooden cross.

Saint Pio's remains are now in the church of Saint Pio, which is beside San Giovanni Rotondo.

References:

Pio of Pietrelcina

en.wikipedia.org/wiki/Pio_of_Pietrelcina

Padre Pio The Man - Biography

www.ewtn.com/padrepio/man/biography.htm

St. Pio of Pietrelcina (Padre Pio) - Saints & Angels - Catholic Online

www.catholic.org/saints/saint.php?saint_id=311

Padre Pio, Cappuchin Priest, Stigmatic

www.padrepio.net/

Padre Pio - Celebrates the Eucharist

www.youtube.com/watch?v=cqLxUExgZVQ

http://www.janson.com/dvd/show_title.php?pid=20238

Padre Pio Shrine

www.padrepioshrine.com/

Padre Pio Shrine, Pantasaph : Home Page

www.padrepio.org.uk/

Library: The Devil and Padre Pio - Catholic Culture

www.catholicculture.org/culture/library/view.cfm?recnum=1021

The Big Question: Who was Padre Pio, and why is he the cause of ...

www.independent.co.uk/.../the-big-question-who-was-padre-pio

Padre Pio (TV 2000) - IMDb

www.imdb.com/title/tt0211559/

Padre Pio: The True Story (9780879736736)

www.amazon.com

Padre Pio Under Investigation - Francesco Castelli : Ignatius Press

www.ignatius.com/Products/...P/padre-pio-under-investigation.aspx

CSI Padre Pio: Wonderworker or Charlatan?

www.csicop.org/si/show/padre_pio_wonderworker_or_charlatan/by AC Friar

Padre Pio site of EWTN, Global Catholic Network

www.ewtn.com/padrepio/index.htm

Padre Pio The Mystic - Stigmata

www.ewtn.com/padrepio/mystic/stigmata.htm

Padre Pio and the Stigmata

www.padrepio.com/app2.html

More From Othniel

Health

5 HTP The Serotonin Connection:
The Natural Supplement that helps you be in control of your mind and body!
ISBN: 1519148445

5-HTP and Depression Management:
Available in Kindle Only

5HTP and Memory Loss Management with:
Available in Kindle Only

5 HTP PMS and Menopause:
Available in Kindle Only

Coping with Arthritis:
ISBN: 151941353X

Coping with BPH:
Benign Prostatic Hypertrophy
Male, over 45, you probably have it!
Available in Kindle Only

Coping with Colorectal Cancer:
Prevention and Cure of theSecond Leading Cause of Cancer Deaths
Available in Kindle Only

Coping with Fibromyalgia:
It's not in your head, it's a disease!
ISBN: 1519438311

Coping with Prostate Cancer:

Prevention and Cure
of Man's Most Common Cancer

ISBN: 1519438737

Heart of a Woman:

Prevetion and Cure of the #1 Killer in Women

ISBN: 1519441533

Heavy and Healthy:

Forget Your Weight and Get Fit!

ISBN: 1519495412

Quit Smoking Now!:

The Program to Help You
Quit Smoking Now and Forever!

ISBN: 1519495781

Sharpening the Aging Mind:

Methods, Tricks & Tips to
Keep Your Mind Super Sharp

ISBN: 1519496028

Sleep Disorders Management:

Available in Kindle Only

The Second half begins at 50:

Your Longevity Handbook

ISBN: 1519496389

Walk!:

Walk Your Way to Great Health & Long Life

Available in Kindle Only

Weight & Appetite Management:

Available in Kindle Only

Relationships:

Adultery Case Histories:
Why People Cheat on Their Partners
Available in Kindle Only
Communing with the Dead:
Death Needn't Part You
ISBN: 1519190085
Foreplay:
The True Focus of Great Sex
ISBN: 1519440979
Sex in the Golden Years:
The Best Sex Ever, Stay Sexually Active for Life
ISBN: 1519495927
The Big O:
Male & Female Multiple Orgasms
ISBN: 1519496109
The Hospice Experience:
Making Your Most Important Final Decision
ISBN: 1519496281
When Your Spouse Dies:
A widow's & widower's handbook
ISBN: 151949646X

Jewish Fiction

Padre Pio:
The Capuchin – the life of Padre Pio -
St. Pio of Pietrelcina
Sex, Horror & Violence vs. Unyielding Faith!
ISBN: 1519495684

Seed of Avraham:

A 4000 Year History of the Jewish Family...

ISBN: 1519495811

Shtetl:

The Story of a Life No More...
As told from the hereafter

ISBN: 1519496036

The Cartographer:

1492

ISBN: 151949615X

The Condemned Voyage:

The S.S. St. Louis - 1939

Available in Kindle Only

The Crusades:

The Jewish World of the 12th Century

Available in Kindle Only

The Death of Berlin:

A Story of Hollocaust Survival and Revenge

Available in Kindle Only

The Remnant:

The Jewish Resistance in WWII

ISBN: 1519496346

The Uprising of Babi Yar:

The Syrets Deathcamp

Available in Kindle Only

Miscellaneous

Guaranteed Routes to Success for Writers:
A Road Map Through Today's Dramatic Changes in Publishing
Available in Kindle Only

Joy of Volunteering:
Working and Surviving in Developing Countries
ISBN: 1519495587

So You Want to Write a Book:
ISBN: 1519496079

If you like this book, please put a review on Amazon.com

Also available in Kindle

Like Otti on Facebook

www.facebook.com/othniel.seiden

Follow Otti on Twitter at

@DTTW5633

#Capuchin

40594344R00146

Made in the USA
Lexington, KY
31 May 2019